Nebendahl   Expert Systems

Expert Systems

Introduction
to the Technology
and Applications

Edited by Dieter Nebendahl

18127-1

Siemens Aktiengesellschaft
John Wiley & Sons Limited

Title of German original edition:
Expertensysteme
Herausgeber: Dieter Nebendahl
Siemens Aktiengesellschaft 1987
ISBN 3-8009-1495-6

British Library Cataloguing-in-Publication Data:

available

Library of Congress Cataloguing-in-Publication Data:

Expertensysteme. English.
    An introduction to the technology and applications of expert systems/editor, Dieter Nebendahl.
       p. cm.
    Bibliography: p.
    Includes index.
    Translation of: Expertensysteme.
    ISBN 0 471 91966 7
    1. Expert systems (Computer science) I. Nebendahl, Dieter.
II. Title.
QA76.76.E95E98913 1988
006.3'3—dc19   88-27844
                                          CIP

Deutsche Bibliothek Cataloguing-in-Publication Data:
Expert systems: introd. to the technology and applications/ed.: Dieter Nebendahl.
[Authors: Klaus Bauer...Transl. into Engl. by Andris Strazds and Edda Norcross]. –
Berlin; München: Siemens-Aktienges., [Abt. Verl.]; Chichester: Wiley, 1988
   Dt. Ausg. u.d.T.: Expertensysteme
   ISBN 3-8009-1513-8 (Siemens-AG) Pp.
   ISBN 0-471-91966-7 (Wiley) Pp.
NE: Nebendahl, Dieter [Hrsg.]

Printed and bound in Great Britain by Butler & Tanner Ltd, Frome and London.

Authors:

Klaus Bauer
Irmgard Büttel
Lutz Eberhard
Margret Hälker
Helmut Lehner
Klaus Micholka
Renate Paulsburg

Translated into English by
Andris Strazds and Edda Norcross, Translation Department,
Siemens Information Systems, Inc., Boca Raton, Florida USA

Production

All texts and graphics of this book were input and formatted with Siemens Office System 5800. The print copy was likewise produced with this system on a Siemens desk-top laser printer, which will be obvious on some pages to experts in this field. The advantages in terms of meeting deadlines and saving costs have been passed on to the reader.

Expert Systems

Preface

Expert systems, as a new generation of software, simulate the problem-solving processes of experts. This means that solution strategies and expert knowledge are represented in a computer program in such a way that problems can be solved quasi-intelligently. But is this really possible?

Yes, scientists and engineers have shown how knowledge can be structured, stored, and recalled, depending on the problem (whether this can be called knowledge processing instead of data processing is left to the reader).

No, if this is to be interpreted as human creativity and intelligence.

There is no doubt that the preoccupation with human problem-solving behavior has given new impetus to programming. New programming methods and procedures have been developed. This book describes these methods and procedures.

The Prologue and Chapters 1, 2, and 3 give an introduction to the subject, and provide the user with basic information about expert systems. Beginning with Chapter 4, new techniques are considered in detail. Knowledge of applied programming techniques will be helpful at this stage.

The Prologue introduces the reader to the subject of expert systems, provides an overview of the problem, and presents the current terminology used with this new software.

Chapter 1 describes the overall research direction from which expert systems emerged, and how these systems are integrated with this research.

Chapter 2 provides information about the areas of application for expert systems, the components that constitute an expert system, the people involved in the creation of expert systems, and the tools used in their development.

Chapter 3 deals with consultations with expert systems, specifically addressing the questions:
Who consults an expert system?
How is an expert system consulted?
When is an expert system consulted?

Chapter 4 considers new techniques for knowledge representation. Representation and handling of knowledge are described based on three techniques employing frames, semantic networks, and production rules.

Chapter 5 presents examples of three programming languages used to implement these techniques.

Chapter 6 describes several shells which facilitate the development of expert systems for specific requirements. The term "shell" is used here in a very broad sense; it also includes programming environments and other aids. This expanded definition serves to distinguish shells from the software which is generally understood by the term "tool".

Chapter 7 describes some of the techniques, based on an expert system game.

Chapter 8 reflects on project experience gained from the expert system SIUX developed by SIEMENS, from the initial planning stages up to the final application.

Special thanks to the authors and colleagues who contributed to this book.

Munich, September 1987

Dieter Nebendahl

Application Software Development
Data Systems Division

Expert Systems

Table of Contents

Prologue

An informative dialogue between

an *Expert* and a **Knowledge Engineer**

A lot is being said and written these days about expert systems.

What exactly are **expert systems**?

By expert systems we mean a new kind of software
that simulates the problem-solving behavior of a
human expert. This software can store knowledge for
a narrowly defined subject area and solve problems by making
logical deductions.

An expert system, then, uses the techniques of **Artificial Intelligence** (AI) ?!

Right!

Expert systems represent one branch of the work being done
in the field of AI.
Computer systems that utilize AI techniques should be able to
relate information intelligently, make inferences, and justify
these inferences (as well as the final result). Expert systems are
typically knowledge-based sytems.

The use of artificial intelligence techniques represents the
transition from data processing to knowledge-based processing.

In what other areas is AI used?

In addition to expert systems, the main application areas are:

- **natural language systems,**
- **computer vision and image processing systems,**
- **robotics.**

Where should expert systems be used?

Wherever a conventional DP solution is not possible
or economical because of the
complexity of the problem, its
dynamics, or the effects of
combinatorial explosion.

These are generally the types of problems that require the use
of **knowledge-based** solution methods.

What do you mean by knowledge-based solution methods?

Knowledge-based systems involve the following:

- **Use of rules or other structures that contain the
  knowledge and experience of experts,**
- **Logical inferences,**
- **Interpretation of ambiguous facts,**
- **Handling of imprecise knowledge, i.e., knowledge
  that is affected by certainty factors.**

How can such a system possibly know everything that I, as an **expert,** *know?*

I have pored over textbooks and attended lectures.

I have accumulated experience by doing the same thing over and over again.
Sometimes I have been successful, and often I have failed.

By spending time and effort, I have learned to be efficient.

I have developed a touch for finding the quickest way to solve a problem and learned how to determine which rules I have to keep and which rules can be disregarded under certain circumstances.

I have built up a number of rules-of-thumb, and know how to apply them in combination with textbook knowledge.

How can my knowledge be available on a computer?

Well, that is my job.

By working together with experts, I try to structure and formalize their knowledge and make it available on a computer in such a way that the computer solves a problem exactly as the expert would.

Empirical knowledge is the hardest to come by, because the experts themselves often do not recognize it as such. It has to be laboriously ferreted out, one precious find after another.

This is why I am called a **Knowledge Engineer**.

So then my knowledge is stored in a database?

No; it is stored in a **knowledge base**.
The knowledge base does not just store facts.
It also contains complex objects, their attributes,
relations between the objects, and rules for processing
knowledge and for deriving new knowledge from
existing knowledge, i.e., **heuristics.**

However, efforts are being made to combine databases,
which contain purely factual knowledge, with knowledge
bases.

How can knowledge be formally represented?

In conventional data processing, knowledge is represented
procedurally, that is to say in the form of algorithms, which
define the individual processing steps needed to solve a problem.
In expert systems, knowledge is represented independently from
the processing mechanisms.

This is known as **declarative representation**.

There are several methods of knowledge representation.

For example:

- **Semantic networks,**
- **Frames,**
- **Production rules.**

Now I know how knowledge is structured and stored in expert systems.
But how does the system know which knowledge is required, when, and how?

The **inference mechanism** performs these tasks. It controls the actions taken by the system. It provides the problem-solving methods by which the rules, networks, or frames are processed.

The inference mechanism in a production rule system, for instance, operates as follows:

- **The facts describing the problem are entered by the user during a consultation.**
- **All rules are identified which could be applied in a particular case.**
- **Conflict resolution strategy is applied, i.e., the appropriate rule is selected.**
- **Execution of this rule and/or activation of new rules.**

All facts describing the problem, as well as the conflict set of rules, the applied rules, newly deduced facts, solutions, and recommended solutions are stored in the knowledge base.

After a consultation, this information can be deleted, or (at least partially) stored as facts.
Thus, the new knowledge acquired while processing a problem can be used again later by the system as "experience."

What kind of **problem-solving** *methods are there?*

The most commonly used methods are:

– **Forward chaining**
– **Backward chaining**

An inference mechanism can also employ a combination of these methods.

In **forward chaining**, you start with the set of known facts and test all the hypotheses in which these facts play a part. In **backward chaining**, you propose hypotheses and try to prove them using the known facts.

So the system solves problems as I myself
would solve them.
As an expert, having participated in the development
on the expert system,
I can trace how the system arrived at a
particular solution.
But how about other users who will consult this
expert system?

In that case, the expert system has an **explanation component**, which provides considerable support to the user during a consultation.

The explanation component provides reasons for the questions asked by the system, justifies inferred facts, and can specify attributes of objects.

The explanation component can also reproduce the solution path and provide reasons as to why other possible solution paths were not pursued.

How does the user communicate with the system?
For example, how can he use the explanation component?

The expert system has a **user interface**.
The question/answer dialogue between the system and the
user during a consultation is conducted via this interface.
It presents the messages from the explanation component
in an understandable form. It is also used for presenting the
result and for the output of system messages.

The expert system also has an **acquisition component**, which
the knowledge engineer uses to implement the knowledge base.

How are expert systems developed?

The ideal method is **rapid prototyping.**
This is an iterative method consisting of the following steps:

– **Concept development,**
– **Knowledge acquisition and implementation,**
– **Testing,**
– **Analysis.**

These steps are repeated until a predefined termination
criterion is met.
In this way, it is possible to create a functional prototype
with a relatively small development effort, and then
gradually improve it.

Development support exists in the form of

- **symbol-processing languages,**
  such as LISP and PROLOG,
- **program development environments,** and
- **shells.**

Symbol-processing languages are especially
suitable for formalized representation of knowledge.
They are interpretative and dialogue-oriented.

Program development environments overlay
programming languages. They provide complex
functions and resources, such as structure-oriented
editors, compilers, debuggers, etc.

Shells are tools which support the work of the
knowledge engineer.

Some are simply tools for structuring knowledge, i.e.,
programs for representing knowledge relationships.
Others provide one or more knowledge-representation
mechanisms, and in some cases an inference mechanism.
Some also offer more extensive control options, or support
the creation of the interface.

Shells already contain all the components of an expert
system, except for the knowledge base.
The knowledge engineer can then concentrate more on
his main task, namely the implementation of knowledge.

Is a shell suitable for every problem area?

Unfortunately not!

Different problem domains require different
problem-solving strategies.
The requirements of the user interface and the
explanation component also vary.
A shell is always developed for a specific problem
area and is therefore not universally applicable.
Furthermore, some shells are available only
on specific computers.

An experienced knowledge engineer will be able to
tell you which shell is appropriate for which problem,
and on which computer.

And where do I find him?

... at Siemens, for example!

*Now that I know something about the design of
expert systems and the tools used to develop them,
can you tell me how a **consultation** works?*

The system asks the user for the facts needed to solve
the problem.

Data input and output may vary a great deal from
case to case.
Using menu technology, the user can indicate the
correct answer on the screen, by clicking a mouse button, for
example. Or, data can be entered from the keyboard.
Help routines provide instructions on how to correct errors.
Explanations by the system can be displayed clearly
with the help of "windows". Many systems also present
information graphically.

*And after I have answered all the questions,
I get the solution?!*

Yes!

One, or more, or perhaps none.

In any case, the reasoning offered by the explanation
component should be considered when evaluating the results.

So the system really does simulate an expert!

Expert Systems

1 An Introduction to AI Technology

1.1 Definition, History

The term "artificial intelligence" is considered a fair, albeit loose description of formal logic techniques, new search procedures and knowledge representation methods used in computer programs. On the other hand, the word *intelligent* seems to imply that experience and insight are inherent in computer programs. These intelligent programs are problem-solving techniques which represent the results of research in human problem-solving methods as well as computers. With this in mind, the following discussion deals exclusively with computer programs, because the engineering discipline involved is the development of application programs for computers. Programming has been a thorn in the side of researchers and developers from the very beginning: it is time-consuming, prone to errors, and difficult to modify.

Researchers and computer experts have always been convinced that more can be gained from computers than what is possible with today's programs. Current development work in data processing continues to be restricted by hardware architecture and "old" programming languages such as COBOL, FORTRAN, and C. These design principles were never intended to produce particularly intelligent responses. On the contrary, the design arose from a combination of programmable calculating machines and communication devices.
This principle is based on the issue of how fast results can be computed and how quickly these results can be transmitted between the individual input and/or output devices. The underlying theories were described by, among others, C. Shannon (information theory), John v. Neumann (computer design principles) and Norbert Wiener (cybernetics).

To scientists and users, however, it was clear that computers were more than communication devices and high-speed calculating machines. This "more," with respect to capabilities, was then deferentially termed "electronic brain." In some applications, man was clearly inferior to the computer in terms of performance. Computers could not only juggle numbers much faster, they could also be used to process and store large amounts of text.

These applications involve large amounts of data with relatively simple processing steps, relieving humans of uncomplicated and/or tedious tasks. Today, the work sequences that can be programmed are getting longer, but also more complicated. The development of new programming languages, software tools, methods, and procedures is not keeping up with the demands of computer applications. The phrase "applications backlog" describes the wish list that cannot be realized due to the apparent lack of development resources. In fact, our methods of solving problems with computers are not effective enough. How does man solve problems? How does the brain work? A little "artifical intelligence" could simplify these problems.

Nevertheless, basic researchers continued to believe that a kind of electronic brain could be implemented with computers.
In the early 1950's, A.M. Turing published *Computing Machinery and Intelligence*. Formal logic and cognitive psychology established themselves as legitimite scientific fields of study. In the early 1960's, A. Newell and H. Simon came out with their book *Human Problem Solving*.

Table 1.1 highlights the most important events in the history of research in the field of artifical intelligence.

Period	Key Events
Pre-World War II roots	Formal logic Cognitive psychology
The postwar years, 1945 - 1954	Computers developed H. Simon, Administrative Behavior N. Wiener, Cybernetics A.M. Turing, "Computing Machinery and Intelligence" Macy Conferences on Cybernetics
The formative Years, 1955 - 1960 The initiation of AI research	Growing availability of computers Information Processing Language I (IPL-I) The Dartmouth Summer Seminar on AI, 1956 General Problem Solver (GPS) Information processing psychology
The years of development and redirection, 1961 - 1970 The search for general problem solvers	A. Newell and H. Simon, Human Problem Solving LISP Heuristics Satisficing Robotics Chess programs DENDRAL (Stanford)
The years of specialization and success, 1971 -1980 The discovery of knowledge-based systems	MYCIN (Stanford) HEARSAY II (Carnegie-Mellon) MACSYMA (MIT) Knowledge engineering EMYCIN (Stanford) GUIDON (Stanford) PROLOG Herbert Simon - Nobel Prize
The rush to applications, 1981 International competition and commercial ventures	PROSPECTOR (SRI) Japan's Fifth-Generation Project E. Feigenbaum and P. McCorduck, The Fifth Generation U.S.'s Microelectronics & Computer Technology Corp.(MCC) INTELLECT (A.I.C.) Various corporate and entrepreneurial AI companies

Table 1.1:   History of Events in Conjunction with Research in Artificial Intelligence.
Source: Harmon, P. and D. King, *Expert Systems*, (New York, 1985),
p. 4.

Let us return to the definition of "artificial intelligence":

Elaine Rich [1] provided the following definition for artificial intelligence:

> "*Artificial Intelligence (A.I.) is the study of how to make computers do things at which, at the moment, people are better*".

In the late 1960's, Alexander Spoerl could often be found working in the data processing research departments of Siemens AG. He wanted to personally slave over programming so that he could explain the functioning of computers to a wide readership. In his book, *Spörl's-Computerbuch* [Spörl's Computer Book], published in 1971, he wrote the following definition of intelligence:

> "Mit Intelligenz meine ich das Vermögen eines Lebewesens oder eines Apparates, Informationen von außen, Beobachtungen, Erfahrungen zu ordnen, Zusammengehörigkeiten zu entdecken, die Informationen damit auszuwerten, das alles, um auf diese Weise Dinge zu abstrahieren, um sie miteinander verknüpfen zu können."

Translation:

> By intelligence I mean the ability of a living being or machine to organize external information, observations, and experiences and to discover relationships that can be used to evaluate the information; all of this is done in order to abstract elements so that their logical links can be established.

The explanation of intelligence in *Meyers Enzyklopädisches Lexikon* [Meyer's Encyclopedia] reads as follows:

> "... die Bewältigung neuartiger Situationen durch problemlösendes Verhalten

Translation:

> "... the mastering of new situations through problem-solving behaviour

which could be completed by adding

> ... on the basis of experience and insight.

The main incentive for the basic researchers was the idea of finding a "general problem solver." This general problem solver would obviate, by a stroke of genius as it were, the tedious step-by-step programming of individual processing steps. This was the initial research approach in the field of artificial intelligence in the U.S.

One approach taken by Siemens in the 1970's was to bypass the programming phase by means of natural-language interaction between man and computer (the Genesis Project).

Neither approach was successful because, as we now know, the initial objectives were exaggerated.

Better methods and procedures are needed to utilize computer tools in problem solving. However, this requires the knowledge and ability to describe human problem-solving behaviour.

Human problem-solving behaviour cannot be explained by considering research in the field of artificial intelligence from the point of view of computer science alone.

It is clear that other areas besides computer science also have important contributions to make. As shown in Figure 1.1, important areas of basic research in artificial intelligence include linguistics, psychology, and philosophy, as well as computer science.

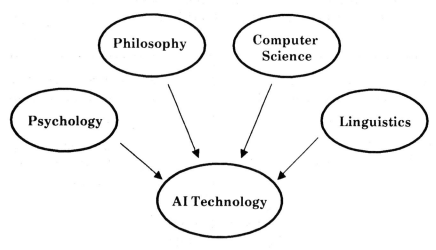

Figure 1.1:   Influences on AI Technology

The individual projects being undertaken in research departments will not be discussed in detail here. A good overview can be obtained from Frank Rose's book, *Ins Herz des Verstandes. Auf dem Weg zur künstlichen Intelligenz.* [Into the Center of the Mind. The Road to Artifical Intelligence.] Rose gives an account of everyday life of the artifical intelligence researcher.

The computer, as a descendant of mechanical calculating machines, has made us feel comfortable with the processing of data (digits, numbers, characters). The more data there were to be processed, the more obvious the power of the computer became. The 1970's and 1980's brought with them the extension of the concept of "data" to "information" (data, text, images, voice), with the term "data processing" giving way to "information processing." Knowledge, however, is the domain of "homo sapiens." Man is intelligent to the extent to which he controls knowledge and uses it, together with his insight and experience, in mastering new situations.

It is in this sense that the concept of intelligence has been transferred to computers, together with the epithet "artificial."

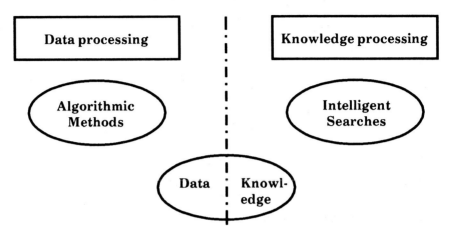

Figure 1.2:   Transition from Data Processing to Knowledge Processing

In other words, the concept of "data" is extended to "knowledge" (objects, relationships, facts, rules, etc.), and the algorithms are extended to include intelligent searches in order to find potential solutions based on this knowledge. In this respect, knowledge processing is an inevitable continuation of data processing development. Researchers and developers realize that it is important to master and combine both techniques (Figure 1.2).

1.2 Branches of AI

From the research efforts described earlier, four areas have crystallized in which preliminary success has been achieved (Figure 1.3).

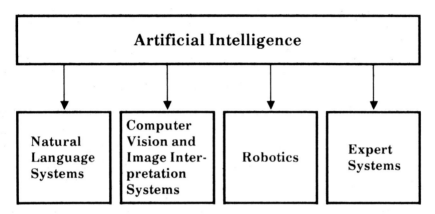

Figure 1.3:   Branches of Artificial Intelligence

These four areas are recognized as branches of artificial intelligence.

This section is intended to provide an overview of natural language systems, computer vision and image interpretation systems, robotics, and expert sytems. Subsequent sections will deal exclusively with the development of expert systems as an advanced problem-solving technique in application software programming.

Natural Language Systems

The focus of language-oriented AI research is to make relevant computer-based applications compatible with natural-language comprehension and to facilitate communication between man and machine.

A system is called a natural-language system if

– part of the input or output information is coded in natural language, and

– algorithms are used for a syntactic, semantic, and pragmatic analysis of the information or for generation of natural language.

The most advanced systems to date are dialog systems, e.g., information systems. Other areas of research include text comprehension (i.e., the system answers questions pertaining to a previously entered text), automatic translation, and generation of abstracts (summarization of text).

Natural-language systems, as opposed to text editors, for example, also have an internal representation for a message. This is necessary for processing the information and for the system to respond in a manner that appears intelligent to the user. After the initial unsuccessful attempts at machine translation and linguistic data processing, the advantages of knowledge-based systems for processing natural language became clear. The generation or "comprehension" of a linguistic expression has three levels:

– Syntactic: the structure of the expression,

– Semantic: the meaning of the expression,

– Pragmatic: the usage of the expression.

This requires knowledge in three areas:

–   General knowledge
    e.g., dictionary, knowledge of idioms, grammatical knowledge, rules
    of dialog or text style

–   Subject-specific knowledge
    e.g., special rules for the specific field, dialog objectives of potential
    users

–   Dialog- or text-related knowledge
    For example, this is knowledge accumulated during a dialog, such as
    information pertaining to the conversation thus far or to the current
    dialog partner.

If the input or output is to be in spoken language, knowledge is also
needed about the phonetics and rhythm of the particular language.

Computer Vision and Image Interpretation Systems

Computer vision and image interpretation systems determine the significance of images on the basis of precisely defined processes. As yet, there are no such systems that are universally applicable. The procedures developed to date are intended only for advanced special applications (e.g., robotics, industrial automation, analysis of aerial photographs).

Computer vision and image interpretation systems generally include the following tasks:

- Division into suitable subprocesses
- Definition of representation forms for intermediate and end results
- Identification and utilization of physical laws
- Identification, representation, and utilization of experience based on knowledge

These tasks require a large number of individual problems to be solved. Processes are needed which recognize intensity of edges, orientation edges, and reflecting edges, i.e., shadows, contours, and color boundaries. Attempts are also being made, for example, to provide extensive general knowledge. Another goal is to develop special hardware which can be used to explore computer-intensive problem-solving capabilities, e.g., interpretation of image sequences.

Areas closely related to computer vision and image interpretation include pattern recognition and image processing.

The main objective of pattern recognition is to detect various distinct features on an object, e.g.,to read letters or numbers.

Image processing includes all computer operations used in the manipulation of image data, particularly those which convert images into other images, e.g., filtering, smoothing, contrast enhancement, geometric rectification, obstruction removal.

Robotics

Robots have engaged the imagination of many people for a long time. The robots used in factories today perform monotonous, repetitive operations according to a precisely defined plan of action.

AI techniques are used in attempts to make the behavior of robots more "intelligent." One example of this would be the robot's response to errors. During the execution of a plan, an unanticipated event may occur. One objective of research is to modify the plan in real time, i.e., during execution, and incorporate an appropriate reaction to the event. If, for example, the robot picks up a screw which is the wrong size, it should be laid aside and another one picked up.

This strategy of generating a practical plan from basic capabilities can also be used in the creation of plans, and not just in their modification.

Additional capabilities are needed if a robot is to be used for non-monotonous work. Robots which are especially mobile require more advanced sensory and visual capabilities.

In order to implement the capabilities mentioned here, as well as additional capabilities, AI techniques are being used more and more in the programming of robots:

- **Spatial** problem-solving techniques,
  3-dimensional space, object geometry;

- **Temporal** inferencing strategies,
  Optimization of motion sequences, coordination;

- **Sensory** processing,
  Selection of relevant information from various sensory data (visual, electronic, etc.);

- **Planning** systems,
  Coordination of spatial, temporal, and sensory information to optimize problem-solving; coordination of several robots in a single production line.

(see also [2] p. A-37)

Expert Sytems

An expert system can, for a restricted subject area, store expert knowledge and solve problems by drawing logical conclusions. The expert system represents the transition from data processing to knowledge processing and, at the same time, replaces algorithms with inference mechanisms.

The groundwork that made these advances possible was the development of programming languages that facilitate the representation and processing of symbolic expressions and complex knowledge structures. This knowledge is stored in the knowledge base and processed with the problem-solving strategies stored in the inference mechanism.

Expert systems are used in those cases where special expertise (specialized knowledge and experience) is available and where a conventional data processing solution is not possible or economical.

This brief overview should suffice at this point, especially since all the remaining chapters deal extensively with this subject.

2 Expert Systems

In this section, expert systems will be presented from the point of view of their applications in the industrial sector. Issues pertaining to basic research will not be considered here. Typical questions directed at application software engineers include the following:

– When does it make sense to use expert systems ?
– What are the individual components of an expert system ?
– How are expert systems created ?

The answers to these questions discussed in the pages that follow are not intended to cover the full scope of the subject, but rather serve to point out specific problem areas that can be satisfactorily solved using expert systems and related techniques .

2.1 Areas of Application

The use of expert systems appears to be appropriate in those cases where experts possess complex knowledge about a highly specific subject area for which no algorithms have been formulated and no complete theories exist.

Another potential area of application includes those cases where theories do, in fact, exist, but where it is not feasible to cover all the theoretically possible cases by means of algorithms within a reasonable amount of time (Figure 2.1).

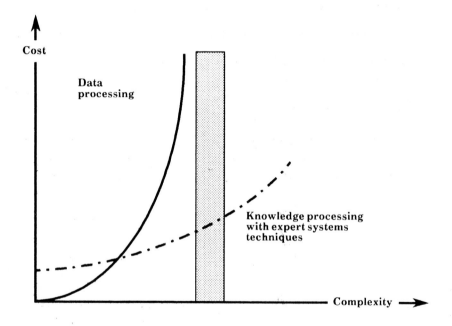

Figure 2.1:   Knowledge Processing Makes It Possible to Overcome the Complexity Barrier

In these situations, the empirical knowledge of the expert is required to arrive at a solution within an acceptable time period.

The two problem areas described above are further characterized in that one or more solutions may, in fact, exist, but the path to the solution(s) is not clearly defined from the outset. The expert, however, frequently finds a solution based on his information about the problem and his experience. Provided that this solution is reproducible and that the problem is clearly stated, the existing set of conditions can be simulated by an expert system.

Because the structuring and implementation of expert knowledge is labor-intensive, the effort required to create an expert system is only justified if that same knowledge will be needed continually over a long period of time by a sufficiently large number of people.

Expert systems offer support in the following ways:

- Errors in complex routine tasks can be avoided.
- Specialized knowledge can be disseminated faster.
- Errors can be diagnosed quickly.
- Planning can be more complete and consistent.

This relieves the human expert of routine tasks, thereby reducing any knowledge bottlenecks. Since the expert's work load is cut back, the number of mistakes is reduced and complex decision-making processes are accelerated.

Table 2.1 provides an overview of current areas of application in various sectors.

Use of Knowledge-Based Systems According to Sector

Sector / Application	Banking, Insurance	Industry	Commerce, Services	Public Sector & Others
Process monitoring and control	• Trend watching	• Process supervision • Process control • Reporting special situations	• Trend watching	• Monitoring of nuclear reactors or large networks (water, gas)
Design		• Configuration • Factories • Product desgin	• Product requirements	• Networks (postal, power supply)
Diagnosis	• Credit deals • Mortgage applications • Risk analysis • Claims processing	• Troubleshooting • Maintenance	• Credit deals • Risk analysis	• Medical diagnosis (hospitals) • Technical diagnosis (power industries)
Planning	• Risk analysis • Securities management • Investment planning	• Design of logical functions • Project planning	• Risk analysis • Market analysis	• Investment planning • Emergency planning • Distribution planning
Consultation services	• Customer service	• Customer service	• Customer service • Specialized services	• Customer service
Training	• Employee training • Field service training	• Employee training	• Employee training • Field service training	• In-house training in legal issues

Table 2.1   Applications of Expert Systems

Expert systems should not be viewed as solutions isolated from other software developments. They are to be incorporated in conventional software when practical. This is particularly true for databases.

Another point concerns the available hardware. In a situation where a system is needed at many different locations, the expert system should run on the hardware available at these locations, if at all possible. While it is true that highly advanced AI machines are available today, they cannot be installed by all users because of the costs involved. With a few exceptions, the expert systems developed on these special machines cannot be used on conventional hardware.

The next sections contain brief descriptions of two expert systems that played a decisive role in the success and continued research and development in the field of expert systems:

- MYCIN   Medical diagnosis expert system
- XCON   Computer configuration expert system

2.1.1 MYCIN

MYCIN is a medical diagnosis expert system that was initiated by E. Feigenbaum and developed by E. Shortliffe and his collegues. Its purpose is to advise physicians on findings and diagnoses in the area of infectious diseases of the blood. The physician's consultation with the MYCIN system begins with a request for general data on the patient: name, age, symptoms, etc. After this information has been made available to the system, the expert system proposes hypotheses. In order to test these hypotheses, the accuracy of the premise part of the rule (see section 2.2.1) must be verified. This is done in one of two ways:

- A search is made for corresponding statements in the knowledge base. These statements, in turn, may also appear in the conclusion part of another rule.

or

– Questions are posed to the user. In this case, the questions are of the type: Has the patient undergone any surgery or other treatment for the urinary tract?

Based on the responses to these questions, MYCIN confirms or rejects the hypotheses.
A series of tests has proved that MYCIN works just as well as the physician.

2.1.2 XCON

XCON is a computer configuration expert system developed by Digital Equipment Corporation.
VAX computer systems are assembled according to individual customer requirements. Because the range of products offered is so extensive, assembling such a system correctly and completely poses an extremely complex problem.

This expert system deals with the following questions:

– Can the parts ordered by the customer be assembled into a functional configuration?

– Are the specified system parts compatible and complete?

The output includes detailed answers to these questions.

XCON can check and process the incoming orders better and faster than the people who did this work previously.

2.2 Components

An important feature of expert systems is the separation of the knowledge itself (rules, facts) from the mechanisms used to process it. In addition, the system has an interface to the user and an explanation component (the procedure involved for a consultation is explained in section 3).

The sections that follow are intended to provide an overview of the individual components. It is not possible to go into too much detail at this point, because the structures of the described components may vary greatly, depending on the specific application.

Components of an Expert System

–	Knowledge Base	The knowledge base of an expert system contains the factual and empirical knowledge of experts in a particular subject area.
–	Inference Mechanism	The inference mechanism of an expert system can simulate the problem-solving strategy of a human expert.
–	Explanation Component	The explanation component explains the problem-solving strategy to the user.
–	User Interface	The user interface employs natural language for dialogs with the user whenever possible.
–	Acquisition Component	The acquisition component provides support for the structuring and implementation of the knowledge in the knowledge base.

2.2.1 Knowledge Base

The knowledge base contains all the facts, rules, and procedures which are important for problem-solving in a specific area of application.

Facts are of the type: The sailing ship "Mary" is 6 m long. This factual knowledge can be represented on the basis of objects, for example. The objects in a knowledge base could then include: ship, motorship, sailing ship. The relationships that exist between these objects are such that a sailing ship possesses all the characteristics of a ship, and in addition, those special characteristics that are unique to a sailing ship. All the characteristics of a ship, e.g., locomotion through water, are described for the object "ship." By means of defined relationships, these characteristics are, at the same time, "inherited" by the object "sailing ship," so that only those characteristics unique to the sailing ship remain to be defined.

This type of programming is called object-oriented programming and is frequently used in the development of expert systems. Certain procedures and functions may have to be assigned to individual objects; for example, speed as a function of wind force and wind direction. The speed is then determined on the basis of these individual data items.

Programs for grouping characteristics and procedures with respect to an object, and the required relationship between the objects, may differ from one application to the next. At this stage, the reader is referred to Chapter 4. Consistency in using the object-oriented approach depends on the problem itself.

In addition to objects, the knowledge base provides rules; these are represented in the form

> **If** premise **Then** conclusion and/or action

In the premise part, questions are asked about the logical links between the characteristics of the objects.

In the conclusion part, new facts and characteristics are added to the knowledge base and/or actions are executed.

This is frequently referred to as rule-based programming.

The following questions arise with regard to creating a knowledge base:

- Which objects will be defined?
- What are the relationships between the objects?
- How will the rules be formulated and processed?
- Is the knowledge base complete with regard to solving the specific problem?
- Is the knowledge base consistent?

These are questions that must be answered by the knowledge engineer, who works with the human expert to the extent necessary.

2.2.2 Inference Mechanism

The inference mechanism represents the logical unit by means of which conclusions are drawn from the knowledge base according to a defined problem-solving method, which simulates the problem-solving process of human experts.

A conclusion is reached by applying a rule to existing facts.

Example

| A rule states: | If p and q, then r |
| The facts are: | p and q |

p and q are precisely those facts specified in the IF part of the rule, i.e., the conditions for the applicability of the rule are given. Applying the rule means: from the facts p and q, conclude the fact r.

A fact exists in an expert system if it is contained in the knowledge base.

The facts specified in the IF part of the rule are called *premises*, and the fact contained in the THEN part is called the *conclusion*. When a rule is applied to any fact(s), we say it *fires*.

The firing of a rule results in the entry of the new (inferred) fact into the knowledge base:

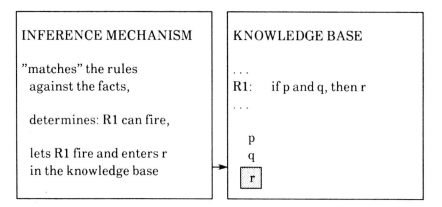

The functions of the inference mechanism include the following:

– To determine which actions are to be executed between the individual parts of the expert system, how they are to be executed, and in which sequence.

– To determine how and when the rules will be processed and, if applicable, to select which rules will be processed.

– To control the dialog with the users.

The rule-processing mechanisms chosen, i.e., the search strategies implemented, are of primary importance in determining the performance of the entire system.

Different problems or different types of problems naturally require different types of inference mechanisms. The inference mechanism must be "adapted" to the problem to be solved. A financially-oriented expert system may require a different knowledge processing strategy than a system intended for machine-error diagnosis.

Further details will not be considered at this point (see section 4.5).

2.2.3 Explanation Component

The solutions determined by expert systems must be reproducible, both by the knowledge engineer during the test phase and by the user. The solutions, of course, can only by verified by the human expert.
There are advantages in knowing, at any point during the system's operation, how far along the system is in processing the problem.

– Which questions are being asked, and why?
– How has the system arrived at intermediate solutions?
– What characteristics do the individual objects have?

etc.

Despite the repeated emphasis on the importance of the explanation component, it is very difficult to meet all the requirements of a good explanation component, and most attempts so far have been only marginally successful. To date, a good explanation component in the German language still does not exist. Many explanation components represent the consultation steps in graphic form. Furthermore, the explanation components attempt to deal with the problem by backtracking through the solution path. It is very difficult to present the found relationships in a clear and understandable (German) text. The existing explanation components may well be adequate for the knowledge engineer, who is very familiar with the specialized EDP environment, and in some cases they may suffice for the experts; but for the user, who often has little or no EDP experience, the existing explanation components are still unsatisfactory.

2.2.4 User Interface

This component determines how the expert system interacts with the user.

- How should questions be answered by the user?
- How will system responses to these questions be formulated?
- What information is to be represented graphically?

The following requirements must be met by the user interface:

- Operation must be easy to learn.
- Erroneous input must be prevented to the extent possible.
- The results must be supplied in a form appropriate for the user.
- The questions and explanations must be understandable.

In the long run, only an interface that is acceptable to users will guarantee the success of the expert system.

2.2.5 Acquisition Component

The work of the knowledge engineer gets considerable support from a good acquisition component. The knowledge engineer can then concentrate mainly on structuring the knowledge, and does not have to devote as much attention to programming.
The acquisition component should have the following characteristics:

- Knowledge, i.e., rules, facts, relationships between facts, etc., must be easy to enter. Frames are often used for the various elements of the knowledge base.

- Easy-to-understand methods of representing all information contained in the knowledge base.

- Automatic syntax checks.

- Continuous access to the underlying programming language.

How the individual requirements are implemented depends on the programming language selected and on the hardware.

The expert should be somewhat familiar with the acquisition component, so that he can make simple changes himself.

2.3 Development

2.3.1 The Development Team

The individuals taking part in the development of an expert system play one of three roles:

– Expert:
  Experts provide the specialized knowledge for the expert system.

– Knowledge engineer:
  Knowledge engineers question the experts, structure the knowledge and use it to implement the knowledge base.

– User:
  Users state their requirements and ideas, and above all, define the scenario in which the expert system will be used.

In the development phase, the main emphasis is on the work of the knowledge engineer and the expert (Figure 2.2.).

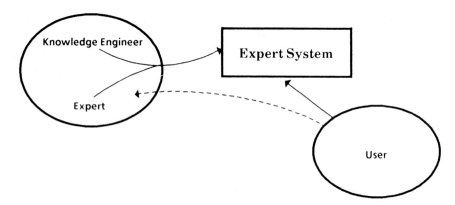

Figure 2.2   Relationships in the Development of an Expert System

The knowledge engineer and the expert work very closely together on the development of an expert system. The first step consists of defining the problems to be solved by the system. Particularly in the first phase of the project, it is very important to correctly identify a specific area of application. The future user, or a representative of the user group, is included in the process at this stage. For the acceptance of the system, i.e., for its success, it is imperative that the user's requirements and ideas be taken into consideration.

Once the area of application has been defined, the expert's knowledge is gradually "fed" into the system. The expert must continuously check whether his knowledge has been transferred correctly. The knowledge engineer is responsible for proper implementation, but not for the accuracy of the knowledge. This is the responsibility of the expert.

If possible the expert should have some understandig of EDP problems. This greatly simplifies the work involved. Also, the developers must never lose sight of the user's requirements during the course of the system's development, so that the final system is of the greatest possible benefit to the user.

It is not always necessary to maintain a strict separation between user, expert, and knowledge engineer. Situations are conceivable in which the expert is also the user. This may be the case, for example, when dealing with an extremely complex subject, where a great deal of time is needed to repeatedly establish relationships and interactions. In these cases, the expert system could relieve the expert of such repetitive tasks.
Usually, the separation between expert and knowledge engineer is maintained.

2.3.2 Development Tools

Efficiency in the creation of expert systems is significantly increased through the use of *shells*.
Simply put, a shell is an expert system that has an empty knowledge base.
The inference mechanism, explanation component, and sometimes even the user interface are in place.

Because the inference mechanism depends on the specific problem or group of problems (see section 4.5), there is no all-purpose shell; rather, an appropriate shell must be selected for each application.

In addition, parts of the inference mechanism may have to be further developed. The extent of these parts will determine whether the use of a shell is still deemed appropriate.
If the knowledge engineer is quite familiar with the shell, i.e., if he knows exactly how the rules are processed, he can then concentrate only on the creation of the knowledge base. The shell often consists of *frames*. These predefined data structures require only that the object name, its characteristics, and the corresponding values, for example, be entered.
The relationships between two objects are represented simply by identifying both objects and the type of relationship. The implementation effort is reduced to a minimum.

The relative importance of frames, explanation components, and/or inference mechanisms varies from shell to shell.

2.3.3 Rapid Prototyping

The development of expert systems involves the following risks:

- There are no comparable examples of implementation which the developer can use as a guide.

- Many requirements are only loosely defined.

The software interfaces and the functionality of components must be defined early in the design and specification phases. In expert system development, these frequently must be changed during and even after implementation, because the requirements have been further developed and have become more precisely defined, or because the situation dictates that other possible solution paths must be explored. Moreover, the path to a final solution can be found and matched to the user's requirements only through individual test implementations during the development phase.

A valuable method has proved to be one in which a prototype of the expert system is implemented, whereby the essential functions of the expert system can be performed, but at a development cost which is considerably lower than that for a conventional implementation. This procedure is called "rapid prototyping." Rapid prototyping is supported to a great extent by specifically developed AI machines, AI programming languages and, if applicable, shells.

Rapid prototyping has proved to be the suitable method for developing expert system; it allows for quick responses to modification requests from both the experts and the users.

3 Consultation

3.1 Users of Expert Systems

Expert systems play the role of intelligent and competent assistants to the expert.

Expert knowledge is usually needed by a relatively large number of people, who generally have no specialized training in the specific subject area.
In this narrowly defined area, there are few experts. The purpose of an expert system is to make the knowledge of these experts available on a continuous basis. The goal is not to replace the experts, or to keep users isolated from the experts, but to provide users with an effective tool, thereby relieving the experts of routine tasks.

In order to use the expert system effectively, however, the user must have sufficient technical knowledge in the specific area. The difference in knowledge levels between the expert and the user should not be too great. Both must be able to "converse" about the problem in a common language using the expert system.

Adding to this situation is the fact that the expert system does not always guarantee a suitable answer. The general circumstances governing the evaluation of the expert system cannot always be covered completely or anticipated. If nothing else, this forces the user to evaluate the relevance of the system response. It is the user who initially bears the responsibility of actions initiated on the basis of a system response. Consequently, the user must be in a position where he can use the explanation facility as a necessary means of control. The problem here is not only the reproducibility of the solution, but rather the ability to understand the interaction of rules under specific conditions.

3.2 Method of Consultation

In the user interface of an expert system, two components are made available to the user:

- an active component, which determines the result by interacting with the user, and

- a passive component, which justifies the result (explanation component).

It is not enough to consider only the active component. If the user were not supported by the explanation component, which enables him to reproduce the path to the solution, it would be very difficult to accept the system response (black box).

The consultation itself generally proceeds according to the following scenario:

First the user is asked several general questions in order to determine the overall context. An initial evaluation based on the knowledge-processing method being used in the expert system then leads to the actual, goal-oriented dialog with the user. On the system side, the dialog is often designed to confirm or reject hypotheses (e.g., verify the cause of an error), or to gradually approximate a predefined objective (e.g., a technically sound configuration of a computer system).

Within the framework of this dialog, the system constantly performs actions which are necessary to solve the problem and to report the system status.

The system responds as an expert would, by

- asking specific questions,

- reporting (in some cases only upon request) intermediate results and modified hypotheses,

- determining the result, e.g., a diagnosis,

- justifying the result, and

- also justifying (sometimes on request only) the rejection of hypotheses.

If required, the explanation component supplies a complete history of the consultation upon completion of the dialog.

It is possible to

- have all user input displayed,

- compare the results obtained with all other possible results,

- have active rules displayed as well as rules which were not applied; active rules which were rejected for the same hypotheses can also be selected and displayed.

The result determined by the expert system depends on the quality of the answers supplied by the user. In general, the expert system cannot check the consistency of user responses. Especially when the user has to make corrections in previously entered information, the system cannot determine what other entered and processed responses may be affected. The consistency of this "metaworld," as far as the system is concerned, is the responsiblity of the user, and not of the system.

3.3   Reasons for Consultation

Consultations are required for many reasons, which depend on the objectives for which the system was developed.

Examples

- Expert-knowledge bottlenecks
- Dynamic reference
- Consistency in consultation
- Confirmation of decisions
- Training
- User support
- Checking personal knowledge

An expert system will be consulted primarily if there is a problem which cannot be solved immediately, and if consulting with a human expert is not a viable alternative at that time. Expert systems also serve the human experts that built them by acting as a *dynamic reference*, which retains knowledge about old relationsships between rules while the experts are turning to new developments. The use of expert systems is also possible at a higher level in order to achieve *consistency and uniformity of consultation* for a large group of people (de facto standardization). A very significant role is played by routine consultations with an expert system for the purpose of positively *confirming a decision*. It is also possible to use such systems for *training*, particularly on-the-job training. Some users rely on system-generated information to reinforce their positions in discussions with other experts. Consultations are also useful for *checking personal knowledge*; the relevance of rule systems is especially well suited to testing with such a system, because, as mentioned before, an expert system can display not only the applicable rules, but also those rules which did not "fire," despite a valid result. In this way, information can be obtained about the sensitivity or robustness of specific sets of subrules.

3.4 Example of a Consultation

The example below illustrates a consultation with the expert system SIUX (see also Chapter 8), a system that analyzes the operation of database applications. The user is first asked several background questions regarding the specific computer system. Then, depending on the responses, the system asks specific questions regarding the problem to be solved.

In other words, a fixed set of questions is not asked in each case; rather, the questions asked depend on the specific situation.

When all of the possible fault isolation options have been considered, the system outputs fault diagnoses.

The other options which are then open to the user can be seen in the example (as translated from a program in German).

```
(OUT)   IF YOU WISH TO CONTINUE AN OLD SESSION,
(   )   PLEASE ENTER THE NUMBER OF THE FILE,
(   )   OTHERWISE PLEASE ENTER 0 :
(   )   0 = DO NOT LOAD FILE
(OUT)   1       TEST                    2       CB
(OUT)
(IN)    0
(OUT)   THE SYSTEM FIRST NEEDS TO ASK A
(   )   SERIES OF BACKGROUND QUESTIONS:
(OUT)
(OUT)   WHICH TYPE OF MACHINE ARE YOU USING?
(OUT)   1   7.530/B    2   7.530/D    3   7.530/F    4   7.531
(   )   5   7.536      6   7.541      7   7.550/B    8   7.550/D
(   )   9   7.550/N   10   7.551
(OUT)  11   7.560/E   12   7.560/F   13   7.560/H   14   7.561
(   )  15   7.570/B   16   7.570/C   17   7.570/G   18   7.570/P
(   )  19   7.571     20   7.580/D   21   7.580/E   22   7.580/I
(OUT)  23   7.580/S   24   7.590/G   25   7.590/R   26   7.738
(   )  27   7.748     28   7.770     29   7.780
```

```
(   )   ANSWER =
(OUT)
(IN)    18
(OUT)   SYSTEM TYPE = 7.570/P
(OUT)
(OUT)   PLEASE ENTER THE CP CONFIGURATION OF YOUR SYSTEM
(   )   IN MB. POSSIBLE VALUES ARE: 2, 4, 6, 8, 10 OR
(   )   BETWEEN 12 AND 128 (IN INCREMENTS OF 4)
(OUT)   ANSWER =
(OUT)
(IN)    16
(OUT)   CP CONFIGURATION = 16
(OUT)
(OUT)   WHAT IS YOUR PAGING RATE? (BASED ON
(   )   SM2 REPORT!)
(OUT)   ANSWER =
(OUT)
(IN)    0
(OUT)   PAGING_RATE = 0
(OUT)
(OUT)   HOW ARE YOUR RESPONSE TIMES ?
(OUT)   1 GOOD      2 AVERAGE      3 UNSATISFACTORY
(   )   ANSWER =
(OUT)
(IN)    3
(OUT)   RESPONSE TIMES = UNSATISFACTORY
(OUT)
(OUT)   HAVE YOU LOADED UDS SHARED ?
(OUT)   1      YES                    2      NO
(   )   ANSWER =
(OUT)
(IN)     1
(OUT)   UDS_SHARED_LOADED = YES
(OUT)
(OUT)   PLEASE ENTER THE NUMBER OF THE DML PER
(   )   SESSION (=15 MIN).
```

```
(OUT)   ANSWER =
(OUT)
(IN)    66200
(OUT)   DML = 66200
(OUT)
( )     ******************************************************
( )     *** THE VALUE FOR DML IS IN THE STANDARD RANGE !  ***
( )     ******************************************************
(OUT)
(OUT)   NUMBER OF LOGICAL_READ DB PER SESSION (=15 MIN) ?
(OUT)   ANSWER =
(OUT)
(IN)    111000
(OUT)   LOGICAL_READ = 111000
(OUT)
(OUT)   NUMBER OF PHYSICAL_READ DB PER SESSION (=15 MIN) ?
(OUT)   ANSWER =
(OUT)
(IN)    3000
   .
      .
   .
      .
   .
      .
(OUT)   THESE ARE THE RESULTS:
(OUT)   >>> FINAL DIAGNOSES
(OUT)   PROBABLE     D91 = DATA BASE_REORGANIZATION_NEEDED
(OUT)   PROBABLE     D52 = LONG-RUNNING_TA
(OUT)   PROBABLE     D41 = DB_DESIGN_INADEQUATE
(OUT)
(OUT)
(OUT)   DATA BASE REORGANISATION NEEDED: PLEASE CONTINUE
( )     ANALYSIS WITH BSTATUS!
(OUT)
```

```
(OUT)  DB DESIGN INADEQUATE: DB DESIGN IS NOT OPTIMAL WITH
(   )  REGARD TO THE PRIMARY PROCESSING SEQUENCE.
(   )  PLEASE CONTINUE ANALYSIS WITH RBAM!
(OUT)
(OUT)
(   )  YOU HAVE THE FOLLOWING OPTIONS:
(OUT)  V = CORRECT ANSWERS               Z = SCROLL
(   )  S = OUTPUT ALL POSSIBLE DIAGNOSES
(   )  ENTER DIAGNOSIS NUMBER -> DISPLAY ALL
(   )  RELEVANT FINDINGS
(   )  B = TERMINATE SESSION
(OUT)
(IN)   D52
(OUT)  SUBSTANTIATION OF D52 = LONG-RUNNING_TA
(OUT)
(OUT)  DO YOU ALSO WISH TO SEE THE UNCONFIRMED RULES
(   )  FOR DIAGNOSIS D52 ?
(OUT)
(IN)   n
(OUT   THE FOLLOWING INFORMATION SUPPORTS THE DIAGNOSIS:
(OUT)
(OUT)  R520   DML/TRANSACTION > 25
(   )  SPECIAL_PROCESSING_ROUTINES = NO
(OUT)
(OUT)
(   )  YOU HAVE THE FOLLOWING OPTIONS:
(OUT)  V = CORRECT ANSWERS               Z = SCROLL
(   )  S = OUTPUT ALL POSSIBLE DIAGNOSES
(   )  ENTER DIAGNOSIS NUMBER -> DISPLAY ALL
(   )  RELEVANT FINDINGS
(   )  B = TERMINATE SESSION
(OUT)
```

```
(IN)    b
(OUT)
(   )   IF YOU WISH TO SAVE THE SUBSTANTIATION OF THE
(   )   DIAGNOSES SUPPLIED, PLEASE ENTER THE
(   )   FILE NAME, IF NOT, ENTER '-'
(OUT)
(IN)    -
(OUT)   IF YOU WISH TO SAVE THIS CASE, PLEASE ENTER
(   )   THE FILE NAME, IF NOT, ENTER '-'
(OUT)
(IN)    -
```

4 Knowledge Representation

Processing and administration of knowledge in an expert system requires that the knowledge be formalized and structured. Generally, the knowledge is made available in the form of case descriptions obtained from interviews with experts, or by observing representative activities.

Formal methods of knowledge representation are forms of logic; e.g., predicate logic, modal logic, multivalue logic, fuzzy logic.

However, these formal mathematical methods are not necessarily suitable tools for communicating with experts in the various specialized fields, nor do these methods offer a universally applicable format for representing knowledge.

Therefore, knowledge representation procedures have been developed which can efficiently support the structuring and processing of knowledge.

These include the following

Production Rules	Based on predicate logic, these describe knowledge in the form of "IF ..., THEN ..." rules.
Semantic Networks	Graphic representation of knowledge based on objects and their relationships.
Frames	Data structures for representing objects.

These procedures, whether in the representation or the processing of knowledge, are based on some form of

Predicate Calculus	Logical deduction based on propositions; a logical conclusion can be drawn if certain conditions are met. The solution can assume the value "true" or "false."

The following sections discuss knowledge representation methods based on

- Production rules,
- Semantic networks,
- Frames,
- Predicate calculus.

These are followed by a description of the methods used in knowledge processing.

4.1 Production Rules

The most comprehensible form of knowledge representation is based on production rules, which are descriptions of condition-dependent actions. A single production rule is understood to be a single item (*chunk*) of information. These chunks of information are the smallest units of information in the entire system.

It has become apparent that experts can best formulate their knowledge in the form of "IF..., THEN..." rules. This is probably the reason why most expert systems today, at least the most successful ones, are based on production rules.

In the implemention of expert systems based on production rules, it soon became necessary to process uncertain knowledge. In these cases, results can be weighted with the help of *certainty factors* (confidence factors). These factors are not to be interpreted in the same sense as confidence factors used in probability and statistics; rather, they are arbitrary weighting factors generally in the range -1 to +1. In this context, -1 could mean "definitely not," -0.5 "probably not," 0 "unknown," +0.5 "probable," and +1 "certain." The value range is continuous in the selected solution space.

Example from the well-known expert system MYCIN, a medical expert system used in the determination of bacterial infectious diseases:

MYCIN

    IF (1) the infection is primary-bacteria, and
        (2) the site of the culture is one of the sterile sites, and
        (3) the suspected portal of entry is the gastrointestinal tract,
   THEN there is suggestive evidence (.7) that the identity of the
        organism is bacteroides

Systems that are set up on the basis of production rules are called *production systems*.

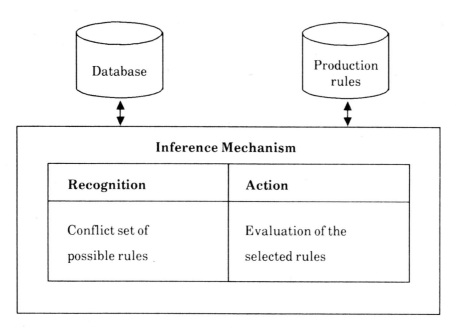

Figure 4.1:   Architecture of a Production System

The most important component of a production system is the inference mechanism. This mechanism controls the processing and the selection of production rules. A good inference mechanism is characterized by efficient methods and conflict-resolving strategies when selecting a rule from a number of possible rules (Figure 4.1).

These methods are discussed in more detail in Section 4.5.

4.2 Semantic Networks

Semantic networks are a means of representing knowledge based on the relationships between objects. The nodes of a semantic network correspond to the objects, and the arcs, or links, between the objects describe the relationships between the objects. Thus, a single arc and its two nodes can be interpreted as a "chunk" of knowledge.

The semantic network, however, provides no information about processing the network. Rules of inference (see Section 2.2.2 and Section 4.5) must still be formulated explicitly!

A semantic network provides a very good overview of the relationships and dependencies in a specific area of knowledge (domain), and is well suited to structuring knowledge and verification by experts. The information contained in the relationships specified by the arcs, however, must be formulated outside of the network.

A semantic network may contain directed relations (dependency of an object relationship) and undirected relations (object relationships); directed relations are represented by an arrow in the direction of the object.

Example of a Semantic Network:

The following relations have been defined:

temp(warm-blooded, mammal)   Mammals are warm-blooded; **temp** is the relation that describes the body temperature.

isa(dog, mammal)   The **isa** relation is a directed relation; every dog is a mammal, but not every mammal is a dog.

isa(cat, mammal)

isa(Spot, dog)   **isa**(Rover, dog)   **isa**(Puff, cat)

home(Maria's_house, Spot)   The **home** relation provides information as to where Spot lives; he lives with Maria.

home(fire_station, Rover)   **home**(Ken's_house, Puff)

color(white, Spot)   Spot is white; the **color** relation assigns the color to the animal.

color(white, Rover)   **color**(black, Puff)

size(60 cm, Spot)   Spot is 60 cm high.

size(40 cm, Rover)   **size**(20 cm, Puff)

between(Maria's_house, fire_station, Ken's_house)
   This relation describes a 3-object relationship. The fire station is located between Maria's house and Ken's house.

The associated semantic network looks like this:

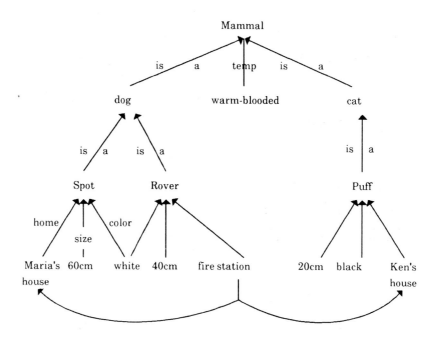

As mentioned earlier, rules which permit additional inferences to be
made must be formulated explicitly outside of the semantic network.
Some examples of such rules are:

$$isa(X, Y) \wedge isa(Y, Z) \rightarrow isa(X, Z)$$

This rule states that if "X" is a "Y" and "Y" is a "Z," then "X" is also
a "Z." In our example: if Spot is a dog and dog is a mammal, then
Spot is also a mammal.

$$size(X, Y) \wedge size(U, V) \wedge (X < U) \rightarrow smaller(Y, V)$$

If both of the size relations are true, and if the first size is less than
the second, then a new relation applies which is not defined in the
network; namely that the first object is smaller than the second
object. In the example, Rover's height is 40 cm and Spot stands

60 cm high, and it is true that 40 cm is less than 60 cm, therefore the following new conclusion can be drawn:
Rover is smaller than Spot. This relation is not found in the semantic network!

isa(X, Y) ∧ R(U, Y) ∧ inheritable(R) → R(U, X)

This rule states: If the **isa** relationship applies to an object and a class, where "Y" represents the class (dog, mammal), and if a rule **R,** applies to this class and this rule can be inherited, then this rule "R" also applies to the object "X" of class "Y."

4.3   Frames

> "A frame is a data structure for representing a stereotyped situation like being in a certain kind of living room or going to a child's birthday party. Attached to each frame are several kinds of information. Some of this information is about how to use the frame. Some is about what one can expect to happen next. Some is about what to do if these expectations are not confirmed."

(Marvin Minsky, 1974)

A frame, therefore, is a means of breaking down objects, or situations, into their constituent parts. These parts are entered in corresponding *slots* in the frame. The slots, in turn, can be subdivided into *facets* (for more detailed structuring).

Example

Conference

Time		
Location		
Subject		
Participants		

Slot   Slot value   Facet

The frame is a predefined data structure, i.e., the frame structure and the slot designations have been defined. In the course of processing, the frames and slots are filled with information. Several frames having the same structure may have different contents.

Conference   Marketing Mtg.

Time	21 Mar 1986 10:00
Location ·	
Subject	*Marketing*
Participants	

Conference   Development Mtg.

Time	21 Mar 1986 10:00
Location	
Subject	*Development*
Participants	

Frames can be used to represent instances, i.e., (object-) class relationships, where *slot-values* can be inherited. This means that only the value in the slot of the hierarchically superior class frame needs to be changed; all subordinate instances of the frames "inherit" the new value.

Example of hierarchical inheritance in the frame concept; inherited values are shown in *italics*:

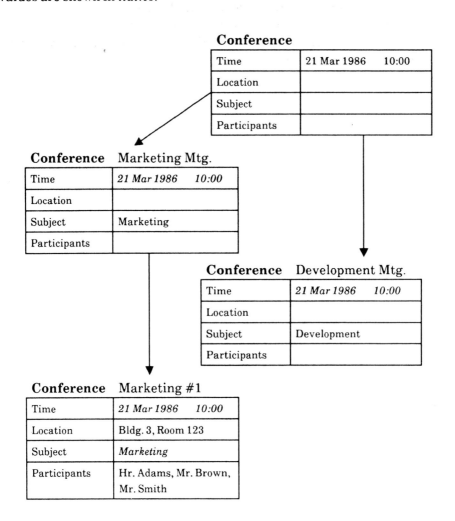

Conference

Time	21 Mar 1986 10:00
Location	
Subject	
Participants	

Conference   Marketing Mtg.

Time	*21 Mar 1986 10:00*
Location	
Subject	Marketing
Participants	

Conference   Development Mtg.

Time	*21 Mar 1986 10:00*
Location	
Subject	Development
Participants	

Conference   Marketing #1

Time	*21 Mar 1986 10:00*
Location	Bldg. 3, Room 123
Subject	*Marketing*
Participants	Hr. Adams, Mr. Brown, Mr. Smith

As with semantic networks, the rules and procedures for processing the frames must be incorporated into the concept. Procedures associated with slots are activated by various events.

If an empty slot is accessed, the value has to be acquired (*if-needed procedure*). In the activated procedure, the value is then either calculated , fetched from the database, or requested by means of a dialog with the user (*user query*), and then entered in the slot.

The value entered into the slot is saved by means of an *if-added procedure*, and deleted by means of an *if-removed procedure*. Both procedures may affect other frames.

Example of possible if-added and if-removed procedures:

slot	slot value	if-added	if-removed

Conference Marketing #1

Time	*21 Mar 1986 10:00*		
Location	Bldg. 3, Room 123		
Subject	*Marketing*		
Participants	Mr. Adams, Mr. Brown		

Participant Adams

Datebook	

Participant Brown

Datebook	

proc **add participant**(conference, participant)

   schedule(conference, datebook (participant))

end

proc **remove participant**(conference, participant)

   cancel(conference, datebook (participant))

   end

The procedure in the example above then appear in the *if-added* and *if-removed facets* of the "Participants" slot.

Systems which operate on the basis of frames offer various processing strategies. The possible strategies, apart from the two detail procedures, are described in Section 4.5.

4.4 Predicate Calculus

Predicate calculus describes knowledge in the form of statements (*predicates*); it is a formal notation used to describe objects and their logical relationships (*relations*), and includes a grammar for generating valid logical statements. Predicate calculus has semantic rules, which relate the symbols of the formal language to the objects, and processing rules, which can generate valid logical expressions from other valid logical expressions.

Predicate calculus, therefore, is a formal language with its own syntax and grammar which can evaluate logical statements and draw conclusions in order to generate further statements.

The programming language PROLOG (see Section 5.1) is extremely well suited for translating the predicate calculus.

Example for predicate calculus:

A total of four statements are given (two facts and two rules). These statements are shown below, represented in both natural language and in their predicate form according to predicate calculus.

Natural language	Predicate calculus

The first two statements are facts.

1. John and Mary are husband and wife.	**husband_and_wife (john,mary)**
Explanation:	*The relation "husband and wife" exists between John and Mary.*
2. Mary lives in New York.	**lives_in (mary, new_york)**
Explanation:	*The relation "lives in" exists between Mary and New York.*

The third and fourth statements involve general rules of inference.

3. If two people (X1 and X2) **husband_and_wife (X1, X2)**
    are husband and wife, they **→ married (X1, X2)**
    are married.

Explanation: *The relation "husband and wife" between persons X1 and X2 implies the relation "married" between persons X1 and X2.*

4. If two people X3 and X4 are **married (X3, X4) ∧**
    married and the person X4 **lives_in (X4, X5) →**
    lives in city X5, then person **lives_in (X3, X5) →**
    X3 also lives in X5.

Explanation: *The relation "married" between persons X3 and X4 and the relation "lives in" between spouse X4 and city X5 implies that the relation "lives in" also exists between spouse X3 and city X5.*

On the basis of these formal statements, the assertion "John lives in New York" can be proved, even though this statement did not previously exist as a fact.

Notation using predicates: **lives_in (john, new_york)**

This assertion is true, if

a) in the conclusion part of a rule, the relation "lives in" is found with two variables that can be linked to "John" and "New York," and

b) in the condition part of the same rule, all conditions that lead to this conclusion have been met.

Expert Systems

In order to prove that the postulated conclusion is true, all assumptions, relations, rules, and facts are compared to one another. If they match without contradiction, the assertion "John lives in New York" is true. If there are any contradictions, the assertion is false. It is also possible, however, that the underlying facts and rules are incorrect - - a problem that always exists.

The hypothesis "John lives in New York," in its predicate notation **lives_in (john,new_york)**, matches the conclusion in the forth statement. The variables "X3" and "X5" are assigned to "John" and "New York" (see diagram).

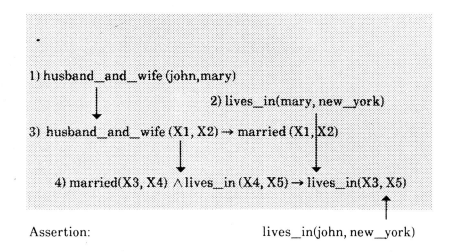

1) husband_and_wife (john,mary)

2) lives_in(mary, new_york)

3) husband_and_wife (X1, X2) → married (X1, X2)

4) married(X3, X4) ∧ lives_in (X4, X5) → lives_in(X3, X5)

Assertion: lives_in(john, new_york)

To test the conclusion in Rule 4, the validity of the two conditions is checked.

The first condition in Rule 4:

married (X3, X4) .   True?

This is not supported by a fact, but it is supported by a conclusion to another rule, namely Rule 3. Therefore, the condition of Rule 3 must also be verified.

Condition of Rule 3:

husband_and_wife (X1, X2)   True?

On the basis of Statement (Fact) No. 1, this condition is satisfied for X1 = john and X2 = mary.

Therefore, the conclusion is also correct:

married (john,mary)   True!

The first condition in Rule 4 is now satisfied for the case:

married (john,mary)

What is now needed is the validity of the second condition:

lives_in (X4, X5)

Since X4 is already linked to the symbol "Mary," the symbol "New York" is assigned to X5 on the basis of Statement (Fact) No. 2. Thus, both conditions of Rule 4 have been met, and the conclusion

lives_in (john,new_york)

is valid.

Although this knowledge did not exist explicitly, it could be determined from the existing statements in the form of facts and rules.

4.5   Inference Strategies

As already shown for predicate calculus, an explicit mechanism must be formulated for processing knowledge. This inference mechanism then evaluates the rules and the facts.

There are two basic techniques for evaluating the rules:

– *Forward chaining*   (forward reasoning)

– *Backward chaining*   (backward reasoning)

Forward chaining is also called *data-driven inferencing* , or the *if-added* method; backward chaining is also called *goal-driven inferencing* or the *if-needed* method.

In both techniques, cases may occur in which there are several rules to choose from:

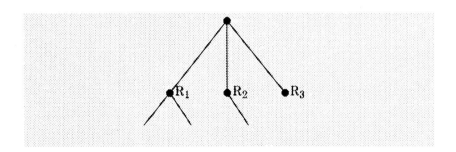

These cases require

conflict resolution for competing rules.

Forward Chaining

In the forward chaining process, the knowledge base is searched for rules that match the known facts, and the action part of these rules is performed. This process continues until either the goal is reached, or until no more rules can "fire" (i.e.,be applied).

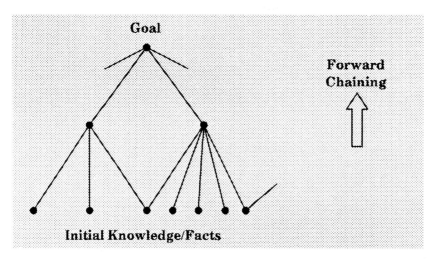

An algorithmic description of forward chaining:

Forward_Chaining (X)

IK: = Initial Knowledge/Facts

UNTIL goal is reached or no more production rules can fire

DO

    (1) Determine the set C of all rules whose premises are satisfied by IK

    (2) Select a rule R from the set C based on the conflict resolution strategy

    (3) IK: = result of the evaluation of R acting on IK plus IK

(Source: W. Wahlster)

Example of Forward Chaining

The knowledge base contains some rules and the known facts. The goal is to generate all facts which can be derived from the knowledge base.

Step 1

INFERENCE MECHANISM	KNOWLEDGE BASE
Matches the rules against the facts,	R1: if p and q, then s
	R2: if r, then t
Determines that R1 and R2 can fire,	R3: if s and t, then u
Selects R1 based on the strategy "The first rule fires,"	R4: if s and r, then v
	p
Lets R1 fire and enters s in the knowledge base,	q
	r
Records that R1 was applied	**s**

Step 2

INFERENCE MECHANISM	KNOWLEDGE BASE
Matches the rules against the facts,	(R1: if p and q, then s)
	R2: if r, then t
Determines that R2 and R4 can fire,	R3: if s and t, then u
Selects R2 based on the strategy "The first rule fires,"	R4: if s and r, then v
	p
	q
Lets R2 fire and enters t in the knowledge base,	r
	s
Records that R2 was applied	**t**

Step 3

INFERENCE MECHANISM	KNOWLEDGE BASE
Matches the rules against the facts, Determines that R3 and R4 can fire, Selects R3 based on the strategy "The first rule fires," Lets R3 fire and enters u in the knowledge base, Records that R3 was applied	(R1: if p and q, then s) (R2: if r, then t) R3: if s and t, then u R4: if s and r, then v p q r s t **u**

Step 4

INFERENCE MECHANISM	KNOWLEDGE BASE
Matches the rules against the facts, Determines that R4 can fire, Lets R4 fire and enters v in the knowledge base, Records that R4 was applied	(R1: if p and q, then s) (R2: if r, then t) (R3: if s and t, then u) R4: if s and r, then v p q r s t u **v**

Step 5

INFERENCE MECHANISM	KNOWLEDGE BASE
Matches the rules against the facts,	(R1: if p and q, then r)
	(R2: if r, then t)
Determines that no more rules can fire,	(R3: if t and r, then u)
i.e., end	(R4: if s and r, then v)
	p
	q
	r
	s
	t
	u
	v

Backward Chaining

Backward chaining starts from a goal, the conclusion (hypothesis). All rules that contain this conclusion are then checked to determine whether the conditions of these rules have been satisfied.

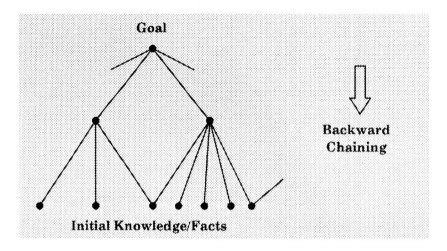

An algorithmic description of backward chaining:

Backward_Chaining(X)

IK: = initial knowledge/Facts

UNTIL Hypothesis (goal) is confirmed or no more production rules can fire

DO

    (1) Determine the set C of all rules whose conclusions are *unifiable* with the hypothesis

    (2) Select a rule R from the set C based on the conflict resolution strategy

    (3) If the premise of R is not in IK, perform backward chaining (premise of R)

Backtracking is possible for Step (2).

(Source: W. Wahlster)

Example of Backward Chaining

The knowledge base contains the same rules and facts as in the example for forward chaining. The goal is to verify the hypothesis "v," i.e., the inference mechanism checks whether "v" can be concluded from the existing facts.

Step 1

INFERENCE MECHANISM	KNOWLEDGE BASE
Checks whether v is contained in the knowledge base,	R1: if p and q, then s
	R2: if r, then t
Determines that v is not in the knowledge base,	R3: if s and t, then u
	R4: if s and r, then v
Postulates v and tries to verify v in the next step.	p
	q
	r

Step 2

INFERENCE MECHANISM	KNOWLEDGE BASE
Matches the rules against v,	R1: if p and q, then s
Determines that R4 has v as a conclusion,	R2: if r, then t
	R3: if s and t, then u
Checks whether the 1st premise of R4 has been satisfied, (i.e. whether s is contained in the knowledge base)	R4: if s and r, then v
	p
Determines that s is not in the knowledge base,	q
	r
Postulates s and attempts to verify s.	

Step 3

INFERENCE MECHANISM	KNOWLEDGE BASE
Matches the rules against s,	R1: if p and q, then s
Determines that R1 has s as a conclusion,	R2: if r, then t
	R3: if s and t, then u
Checks whether the 1st premise of R1 has been satisfied, (i.e., whether p is contained in the knowledge base)	R4: if s and r, then v
	p
Determines that p is in the knowledge base ,	q
	r
Checks whether the 2nd premise of R1 has been satisfied, (i.e., whether q is in the knowledge base),	s
Determines that q is in the knowledge base ,	
Determines that all premises of R1 are now satisfied,	
Lets R1 fire and enters s in the knowledge base.	

Step 4

INFERENCE MECHANISM	KNOWLEDGE BASE
As a continuation of Step 2, checks whether the 2nd premise of R4 has been satisfied, (i.e., whether r is contained in the knowledge base)	R1: if p and q, then s
	R2: if r, then t
	R3: if s and t, then u
	R4: if s and r, then v
Determines that r is in the knowledge base ,	p
	q
Determines that all premises of R4 are now satisfied,	r
	s
Lets R4 fire and enters v in the knowledge base	v

Step 5

INFERENCE MECHANISM	KNOWLEDGE BASE
As a continuation of step 1, concludes that the hypothesis v has been verified.	R1: if p and q, then s
	R2: if r, then t
End.	R3: if s and t, then u
	R4: if s and r, then v
	p
	q
	r
	s
	v

Unification

The process of matching structures by linking values to variables is called *unification* (see also section 5.1.2).

Backtracking

If unification is not possible, value-to-variable links must be cancelled for this production. The inference mechanism then tries to find another rule with which to achieve unification. This process of cancelling the value links, i.e., backing up, in order to allow another rule to be selected, is called *backtracking*.

Blackboard Architecture

Blackboard systems use an information pool into which facts and states are entered. Event-driven procedures, called *demons*, act on this information pool, i.e., the blackboard. These demons are activated in the blackboard by events, and utilize this information to perform their actions. The demons, in turn, enter their results in turn in the blackboard.

Blackboard architectures are complicated to use. A well-known system employing blackboard architecture is HEARSAY; this system can process voice input using natural language.

The example described in Chapter 7, EXPS.MASTERMIND, is implemented with blackboard architecture.

Conflict Resolution with Competing Rules

The possible selection strategies are shown below:

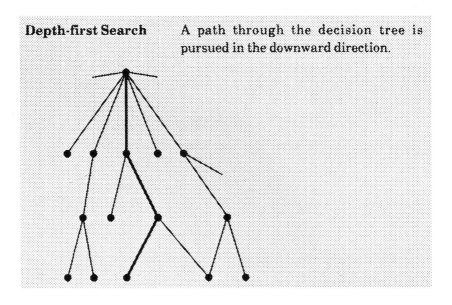

Depth-first Search   A path through the decision tree is pursued in the downward direction.

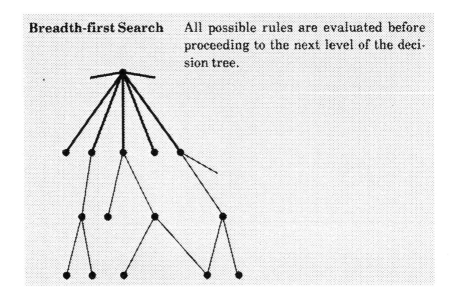

Breadth-first Search   All possible rules are evaluated before proceeding to the next level of the decision tree.

The strategy used depends on the specific problem and on the knowledge engineer's instincts. The depth-first strategy should be used in cases involving a restricted search space, in order to obtain a result as quickly as possible. The breadth-first search strategy is more of a groping approach toward a solution. Generally, a combination of the two strategies is used.

Other possible selection strategies used when several rules can be applied at the same time include the following:

- Select the rule that has the strongest influence on the hypothesis which is currently the highest rated;

- Select the rule which involves the least effort to determine the necessary facts;

- Select the rule whose facts can be determined with the least amount of risk;

- Select the rule that reduces the search space the most;

- Select the rule for which most of the conditions are already known;

- Select the rule which provides an acceptable query/response exchange with the user;

- etc., ...

5   Programming Languages and Systems

Expert systems can be developed in any programming language. However, some languages are particularly well suited because of their underlying concepts. Programming languages are generally classified according to the various programming paradigms.

Below is a brief summary of programming paradigms :

- *Procedure-oriented programming paradigm*
  This is known as algorithmic programming. A program consists of the description of the processing sequence.

- *Declarative programming paradigm*
  In this paradigm, a problem is described using facts and rules. In the strictest sense of the paradigm, no procedural sequences may be formulated.

- *Functional programming paradigm*
  In this case, a problem is solved via systematic application of functions. A function, when performed, supplies a value which is then further processed by the calling function. If the functional paradigm is used consistently, no value assignments are ever required in a program.

- *Object-oriented programming*
  Object-oriented programming is based on the description of objects; these objects send messages to (other) objects and apply methods when messages are received. These methods can send additional messages and/or cause changes in the status of the object.

The languages most frequently used in the development of expert systems and shells are PROLOG and LISP.

PROLOG is a declarative language in which knowledge can easily be represented in the form of production rules.

LISP is a functional language which, like PROLOG, has the following advantage:
Emphasis is placed more on manipulating symbols and structures than on numerical computation. Furthermore, no distinction is made between the structure of data and programs.

Additional support is provided by shells, which are commercially available and offer a variety of features (see Chapter 6). Shells are generally based on PROLOG or LISP.

As an example of the object-oriented programming paradigm, Chapter 6 (Shells) contains a description of LOOPS, an extension of Interlisp-D.

Programming systems such as Interlisp-D represent a transition to the shells.

Hardware environments for expert system development are frequently built around "dedicated" machines. Their microcode is developed with the programming language in mind. At present, such machines are commercially available only for the LISP language .
PROLOG machines are primarily being developed within the framework of the "Fifth-Generation Program" in Japan and in England. They are not yet available to the general public. Dedicated machines are intended to be used as workstations.

The sections that follow describe the PROLOG and LISP languages, as well as the Interlisp-D programming system.

5.1 PROLOG

The name PROLOG is an acronym of **Pro**gramming in **Lo**gic, which is a reference to the origin of the language: it is an implementation of first order predicate logic as a programming language.

PROLOG is currently being used as a development language for AI applications in various projects in Europe. Japan's objective in the Fifth-Generation Project is to develop a logical programming language based on PROLOG and parallel processing hardware that understands this language. In the United States, LISP is used more frequently than PROLOG; for most AI workstations, PROLOG is offered as well.

DECsystem-10 PROLOG, created in Edinburgh, and the version of PROLOG described in the book *Programming in PROLOG* by W.F. Clocksin and C.S. Mellish [6] have established themselves as quasi- standards. Most PROLOG dialects are based on these two versions and the scope of their language includes DECsystem-10 PROLOG.

Programs written in PROLOG are interpreted differently than those written in LISP (and other languages). Kowalski wrote an article on this subject entitled "Algorithm = Logic + Control" [7]. In this article, the author shows that the logic component in algorithms can be separated from the control mechanisms.

The logic is represented in the form of predicates, which appear in three forms: as facts, rules, and questions. The logic formulated as facts and rules is designated the knowledge base. The questions are then directed at this knowledge base.

These queries are processed by the so-called *theorem prover*, which checks whether the predicate to be proved can be deduced from the knowledge base. The theorem prover is part of the PROLOG interpreter and represents the control mechanism, which consists of unification and backtracking (see Section 5.1.2). The programmer then needs to do little more than design the logic of a program, and no longer has to program the individual computing steps. This type of programming is called declarative, as opposed to the conventional procedure-oriented programming.

In the next sections, other important concepts will be discussed and illustrated by means of examples. The sample program is followed by a brief description of syntax and semantics, a user dialog, and an explanation of the essential mechanisms of PROLOG. The conclusion summarizes the most important PROLOG characteristics.

The theoretical basis of PROLOG (predicate logic, resolution principle, and Horn clauses) will not be discussed in detail here. Such a discussion is not necessary for a practical understanding of PROLOG, and would contradict the introductory nature of this section. Those interested are referred to Chapter 4, Knowledge Representation, in this book and Chapter 10 in Clocksin/Mellish [6].

5.1.1 Syntax and Semantics

The description of PROLOG syntax in this section is restricted to those parts necessary for the sample program in Section 5.1.3. and, therefore, does not represent the full range of PROLOG syntax and semantics.

The sample program in Section 5.1.3 contains five predicates. The predicates consist of one or more clauses (**free**(...) consists of five clauses). A *clause* (also called a Horn clause) always extends from the *predicate name* (**free**) up to the terminating period. A clause can be a *fact*:

```
free('15569').
```

or a *rule*:

```
move(From, To):-
    decide (From, To, Reasons)
    print_move(From, To, Reasons).
```

A rule consists of the *head* (**move(From,To)**) and the *body* (**decide(From,To,Reasons),print_move (From,To,Reasons)**), separated by "**:-**". A fact has only one head.

The symbol "**:-**" stands for a logical implication, but one which works in the opposite direction: if the body is true, then the head is also true. A fact is therefore always true, since it has no conditions. A body is true if each of its parts is true.

A predicate name, together with the list of its parameters in parentheses, is called a *structure.*

> **decide(From, To, Reasons),**

In addition to the predicate name, every predicate has a fixed number of parameters.

Symbols which begin with a lower-case letter or which are enclosed in single quotes are constants:

> **free , 'AA 73'.**

Symbols which begin with an upper-case letter are variables. Variables used in a clause are local, i.e., they have different meanings in other clauses:

> **From, To, Any.**

The data structure used most often in PROLOG is the list. A list consists of the opening square bracket "[", the list elements, which are separated by commas ",", and the closing square bracket "]":

> **['is bigger', ' has better layout'].**

A list element can itself be another list.

5.1.2 Important Mechanisms

Important mechanisms used in PROLOG include: recursion, instantiation, verification, unification, backtracking, and interchangeability of unknowns.

Recursion represents the most important program structure. Branches and FOR loops are not provided in the PROLOG syntax, and WHILE loops are very difficult to implement, since variables can be linked only once. Recursion is more suitable than other program structure for processing recursive data structures such as lists, and is characterized in these cases by simpler representation and better clarity.

Instantiation is the linking of a variable to a constant or structure. The linked variable then behaves like a constant.

Verification denotes the attempt to derive from the knowledge base (facts and rules) the structure of a query which is to be proved. If this is possible, the structure is true, otherwise it is false.

Unification is the main component in the verification of structures. A structure is proved if it can be unified (matched; see below) with a fact, or if it can be unified with the head of a rule, and the structures in the body of this rule can be verified.

Example of Unification (see also Section 5.1.3)

The structure **"free(X)"** can be unified with the fact **free('15569')** and is thus proved. The structure **move(X,Y),** on the other hand, can be matched only with the clause head **move (From, To)**, and is only satisfied if the clause body has also been verified.
An attempt is now made to prove **decide(From, To, Reasons)** and **print_move(From, To, Reasons)**.

How, then, does the unification of two structures work? The set of facts and rules is searched from the top down in the sequence in which they are written, until a fact or a clause head is found which belongs to the same predicate as the fact which is to be proved. The individual parameters are then checked in pairs to determine whether they match: two constants must be identical, two variables are linked to one another, a variable assumes the value of the constant.

After the unification of **free(X)** with **free('15569')**, X has the value '15569'. In other words, X is instantiated to '15569'.

In the verification of a structure, it is possible that this structure cannot be unified with a found structure of the same predicate. In such a case, the knowledge base is searched further for a suitable fact or rule head which can be unified. If none can be found, the structure is not verifiable. If the structure to be proved is the goal of a query, the query is answered in the negative. If, on the other hand, it is only part of a clause body, then the links (instantiations) established in the preceding structure of the clause body are cancelled and another attempt is made at unification. This is followed by an attempt to verify the second structure.

This process of cancelling instantiations and backing up in the computation when verification fails is known as *backtracking*.

Expert Systems

Interchangeability of unknowns is illustrated in the user dialog of Section 5.1.4. In contrast to procedures written in other programming languages, such as PASCAL, predicates in PROLOG do not define which parameters are input parameters, output parameters, or transient parameters. A predicate behaves in different ways, depending on whether a parameter is a variable or a constant:

> **move ('LZ 2669', 'CC 08')** determines the reasons for a move. If 'CC 08' is not a suitable room, the answer is **not verifiable**.

> **move ('LZ 2669', New_room)** supplies the set of suitable rooms, together with the respective reasons.

> **move (Old_room, 'CC 08')** finds all rooms for which a move to room 'CC 08' would be an improvement.

This example also illustrates the difference when compared to procedure-oriented programming. Procedure-oriented programming would require three different procedures for these actions.

Backward chaining is implemented in the PROLOG control mechanism. A rule **IF A and B and C then D** corresponds to the PROLOG clause **D:-A,B,C**. However, this backward chaining is normally too weak to process rules for an expert system, since there are no control options for rule interpretation, nor trace facilities.

In spite of its declarative character, PROLOG does possess *control structures*. In some cases it is desirable or even necessary to prevent backtracking within a part of a predicate. This is made possible through the use of the pseudo-predicate '!' (pronounced "cut"). During backtracking, instantiations before the '!' are not cancelled; instead, the predicate is abandoned immediately.

5.1.3 Sample Program

Below is an example of a program for determining a suitable room to move to. A room is considered to be suitable if there is no better room available. Because not all rooms can be compared to one another, there may be several suitable rooms.

The program contains five predicates:

move, decide, print_move, free and **better**.

The facts given are the free (available) rooms and a comparison of rooms (predicate **better**).

```
free('BB 64').
free('AA 73').
free('15569').
free('CC 08').
free('DD 62').

better( 'BB 64', 'LZ 2669', ['is bigger', 'has better layout']).
better( 'AA 73', 'BB 64',  ['is on the sunny side']).
better( 'CC 08', 'BB 64',  ['is bigger','has better view']).
better( 'DD 62', 'LZ 2669',['is closer to elevator ',' has coffee
                            machine']).
better( '15569', 'AA 73',  ['is closer to cafeteria']).
```

The last predicate states: Room '15669' is better than Room 'AA 73' because it is closer to the cafeteria. In all other respects, the two rooms are identical. The predicate is transitive; i.e., 'AA 73' is better than 'LZ 2669', because 'AA 73' is better than 'BB 64' and 'BB 64' is better than 'LZ 2669'. The reason for the superiority of 'AA 73' is then the union of both sets of reasons ['is bigger', 'has better layout', 'is on the sunny side'].

The most important predicate is **move**; it determines the reasons for a move with the help of the predicate **decide**, and prints out the result with **print_move**.

```
move(From, To):-
    decide( From, To, Reasons),
    print_move( From, To, Reasons).
```

decide tests whether a room is suitable for a move, and records the reasons in favor of this room.

```
decide( OldRoom,NewRoom,ReasonsForNewRoom):-
    free(AnyRoom)
    better( AnyRoom,OldRoom, Reasons1),
    decide( AnyRoom,NewRoom, Reasons2),
    append(Reasons1, Reasons2, ReasonsForNewRoom).
```

A search is made for a free room (AnyRoom), a test determines whether this room is better than the old room (OldRoom), and the reasons in favor of this free room are recorded in Reasons1. The predicate **decide** is then applied recursively to this free room, and a search is made for a room that is more suitable than the free room. The reasons for the new, more suitable room are represented by the union of the reasons for the free room and the reasons from the recursion. The auxiliary predicate **append** is needed to concatenate these two lists.

```
decide( Room, Room, [ ]):-
    free(Any),
    not (better(Any, Room, Reason)).
```

This second case ends the recursion: for all free rooms (Any), it is true that they are not better than Room. If that is the case, then the suitable room is Room (the second parameter of **decide**). There are no additional reasons in favor of this room.

print_room is a predicate used to output the result:
It prints out the old room, the new room, and the reasons for a move.

write and **nl** are built-in predicates, i.e., they are already incorporated into the system.
write prints the value of a constant or variable; **nl** causes a line feed.

```
print_move ( From,To,Reasons ):-
    nl,
    write( "A move from room "),
    write( From),
    write("to room"),
    write(To),
    write("is supported by the following reasons:"),
    nl
    write( Reasons),
    nl.
```

5.1.4 Dialog Using the Sample Program

The following dialog took place on a Siemens Personal Computer PC-MX2 with SIEMENS-PROLOG.
A query begins with the predicate name, followed by a structure to be proved, and ends with a period '.'.

In this example, the symbol "?-" is the interpreter's prompt.

There are three possible system responses to a question: **verifiable, not verifiable**, or the value of the variable sought.

If the system outputs the value of the variable sought, the cursor remains positioned at the end of the output.

The user can then

– press the "Return" key to end the query;

– enter the character ";" and press the "Return" key to continue the search for further values.

The following queries would be possible for our example:
(**user input** is **shaded**)

?- **free('BB 64').** **verifiable**	User: Is Room 'BB 64' free? System: Yes
?- **free('LZ 2669').** **not verifiable**	U: Is room 'LZ 2669' free? S: No, the corresponding fact is not in the knowledge base.
?- **free(X).** **X = 'BB 64'** ;	U: Which rooms are free? S: Room 'BB 64' is free. U:Continue search
X = 'AA 73' ;	S: Room 'AA 73' is also free.
X = 'DD 62' ;	.
X = 'CC 08' ;	.
X = '15569' ;	. U:Continue search S: There are no other free rooms.
?- **better('AA 73', 'LZ 2669',Reasons)** **not verifiable**	U:Is Room 'AA 73' better than Room 'LZ 2669'? S: No, there is no such fact, nor can it be deduced.
?- **better('BB 64', 'LZ 2669',Reasons).** **REASONS = ['is bigger', 'has better layout']** ;	U:Is Room 'BB 64' better than Room 'LZ 2669'? S: Room 'BB 64' is better because it ['is....] .
not verifiable	U:Continue search S: There are no other reasons.

?- move('LZ 2669' , 'CC 08').
A move from room LZ 2669
to room CC 08 is supported
by the following reasons:
[is bigger, has better layout,
has better view]
verifiable

U: Is Room 'CC 08' a suitable replacement for Room 'LZ 2669'?

The predicate print_move
outputs this text.
S: Yes

?-move('LZ 2669' , NewRoom).
A move from Room LZ 2669
 to Room 15569 is supported
'by the following reasons:
[is bigger , has better layout,
is on the sunny side, is
closer to cafeteria]
NewRoom = '15569'   ;

U: Which rooms are better than
'LZ 2669' ?

:

The predicate print_move
outputs this text.

S: A possible new room is
'15569'
U: Continue search

A move from Room LZ 2669
 to Room CC 08 is supported
by the following reasons:
[is bigger, has better layout,
 is bigger, has better view]

The predicate print_move
outputs this text.

NewRoom = "CC 08'

S: Another room is 'CC 08'

verifiable

U: Presses the "Return" key,
ending the current query.

?-move(OldRoom,'CC 08').

U: For which rooms is Room 'CC 08' a more suitable alternative?

A move from Room LZ 2669 to Room CC 08 is supported by the following reasons:
[is bigger,has better layout, has better view]

The predicate print_move outputs this text.

OldRoom = 'LZ 2669'   ;

S: Room 'CC 08' is a suitable alternative to Room 'LZ 2669'.
U: Continue search

A move from Room BB 64 to Room CC 08 is supported by the following reasons:
[is bigger,has better view]

The predicate print_move outputs this text.

OldRoom = 'BB 64'

S: Room'CC 08' is also a more suitable room than Room 'BB 64'.

verifiable

U: Presses the "Return" key, ending the current query.

5.2 LISP

The name LISP stands for **List** Processing, owing to the fact that LISP was developed for the processing of lists. The list is the most important structure in LISP. Over the years, many dialects have been developed such as MACLISP, COMMONLISP, INTERLISP and ZETALISP. Of these, COMMONLISP has emerged as a standard.

This section contains an introduction to the LISP language. More extensive features offered by LISP systems are described in Section 5.3, INTERLISP-D.

The following characteristic concepts are implemented in LISP:

Lists and Atoms

– The most important structure is the list, as indicated by the name "LISP" - List Processing.

– Atoms can be assigned properties (see Section 5.2.1).

The 'Function'

– Every LISP function and every LISP program has a list structure. Syntactically, programs cannot be distinguished from data.

– LISP has its own basic functions (see Section 5.2.2).

Mode of Operation

– LISP is a functional language.

– Recursion function definitions are possible.

– Procedure linking is dynamic, i.e., it takes place at the time of execution, not during linking or loading, as with other programming languages.

– Dynamic memory management is carried out automatically by the system (see Section 5.2.3).

5.2.1 Lists and Atoms

The list is the basic structure of LISP. Lists are constructed as follows:

$(l_1\ l_2\ ...\ l_n)$,   where l_i can be either another list or an atom.

Example

(A (B C) D) is a list containing three elements;

A	Atom
(B C)	List consisting of the atoms B and C
D	Atom

An empty list, **"( )"** or **"NIL"**, is also valid.

This format makes it possible to create structures of any complexity.

Atoms can be numbers, strings, or symbols, e.g.,: 5, *"This is a string"*, *symbol*.
A symbol - like a variable in other programming languages - can take on values, e.g., a number, or it can be the name of a function, or both. In the last case, the context determines whether the value or the function is used (see Section 5.2.2).

A symbol can also be assigned properties, which include additional information besides the value of the symbol. These properties are also referred to as attributes.

Example

(The function of the character will be explained in Section 5.2.3.)

R5 is a symbol.

The function PUTPROP can be used to store information, e.g., about price and origin:

(PUTPROP 'R5 'price 'inexpensive)
(PUTPROP 'R5 'origin 'foreign)

(See next section for syntax).

Example

The function GETPROP supplies the value of a property as the result. The question on the origin of R5 has the format:

(GETPROP 'R5 'origin)

and the result is:

foreign.

With the help of the properties, LISP makes it possible to store and process knowledge in a structured form.

5.2.2 The 'Function' in LISP

Every LISP program consists of function calls. The function calls have a list structure, i.e.,

$$(\text{FN } [\text{Arg}_1 \, [\text{Arg}_2 [\, ... \,]]])$$

The first element is the function name (FN in the example above). Any additional elements (such as Arg_1, Arg_2) that follow the name are the arguments to which the function, symbolized by the function name, is applied.
If no other elements follow, the function is simply executed.
The arguments can be atoms or lists:

$$(\text{FN } \text{Arg}_1 \, (\text{Arg}_3 \, \text{Arg}_4))$$

The list (Arg_3 Arg_4) can itself be another function call. In this case Arg_3 would be the function name and Arg_4 the argument to which the function Arg_3 is applied.

Lists that represent a function call are syntactically not different from lists that are processed as data.

LISP provides several basic functions for list processing, e.g.,:

CAR Function

The **CAR** function returns the first element of a list as the result.

The LISP program
(CAR '(A B C))
returns the result
A.

CDR Function

The **CDR** function removes the first element of a list.

(CDR '(D E F G))
returns the list
(E F G).
as the result.
This is called the *rest* of the list (**D E F G**).

In addition to the list processing functions, LISP provides arithmetic functions, input/output functions, and assignments, among other things. Control structures, which control the execution of a program, are also defined, e.g., conditional expressions. Loops do not exist explicitly . They can be implemented by recursion or by means of so-called **MAP** functions.

MAP functions process lists from beginning to end. The **MAPCAR** function, for example, applies a user-defined function to the elements of a list, and combines the results again to form another list.

Example

(MAPCAR '(2 -4 6) 'MINUS)

returns as the result the list

(-2 4 -6)
(The **MINUS** function forms the negative of a number.)

Many LISP systems also provide supplementary constructs, such as **FOR** and **WHILE** loops.

5.2.3   Mode of Operation of a LISP System

Evaluation of Lists

The LISP system reads in each user input, evaluates it, outputs the result, and waits for the next input (READ-EVAL-PRINT loop).

The user can input atoms or lists, whereby each list is interpreted as a function call. The value of atoms is either the atom itself, in the case of numbers and strings, or, in the case of symbols, the value of the symbol, e.g., 5, if the entered symbol has the value 5.

The value of a list is calculated by evaluating each element of the list.

The first element must be a symbol and serves as the name of the function. The associated function is then applied to the remaining list elements , i.e., the arguments.

If the remaining list elements include yet another list, this list is treated and evaluated as a function call. The result then serves as an argument for the superordinate function.

If a function supplies a list as a result, this list is considered the value of the function call, not another function call.

The quote character " ' " is a function itself, but one which deviates from the above rule. It prevents the evaluation of a list or a symbol which is to be used as an argument of a function. In other words, the QUOTE function returns its arguments unchanged as the result. For example, **(QUOTE X)** or **'X**, returns **X** as the result.

Examples of the QUOTE Function

1) The result of
(CAR '(A B C))
is
A,

because **CAR**, being the first element in the list, is considered a function, and the list **(A B C)** the argument of this function. **CAR** is defined as a function which returns the first element of a list, so the result is **A**.

2) It is assumed that there is no function with the name **A**.

The attempt to evaluate
(CAR (A B C)) (without a quote preceding **(A B C)**)
then fails, because **A** is not the name of a function.

3) **(CAR (CDR '(A B C)))**, on the other hand, can be evaluated:

The function **CAR** is applied to the result of the list
(CDR '(A B C))
i.e., the list with the value **(B C)**;
this list is not another function call.

(A B C) is not evaluated, because of the " ' ".

Therefore
(CAR (CDR '(A B C)))
has the value
B.

4) If the value of the symbol **L** is the list **(A B C)**, then

(CDR L)

can also be evaluated.

In the evaluation, the value of **L** is determined first, i.e., **(A B C)**; then the "rest" **(CDR)** of **(A B C)**, i.e., **(B C)**, is calculated.

However, this list evaluation procedure is often not followed. For example, there are functions whose arguments are not evaluated. In these cases, the quote character is unnecessary (and even <u>illegal</u>).

User-defined Functions

Users of LISP systems can also define their own functions. Recursive function definitions are allowed, and are extremely useful when working with the recursive structure of the lists.

When a new function is defined, it is integrated into the LISP environment and is available at any time, just like the predefined functions with regard to application.

Procedure Linking

A function is linked only at the time it is called, not during the linking or loading phase, as is the case with other programming languages.

Therefore, the most up-to-date definition of a function is always accessed. However, this also means that a function which is called several times within a program can be modified (redefined) by the program between two calls. For the next call, the modified function is executed, since it is now the most up-to-date definition.

Thus, a LISP program itself can create or modify a program, or parts of a program, and then initiate execution.

Components of a LISP System

An important component of a LISP system is the dynamic memory management. The system allocates the memory space for the constantly changing lists,without explicit requests from the user. Memory areas which are no longer required are deallocated by the system for subsequent use elsewhere (garbage collection). This is necessary because of the basic structure of LISP, i.e., the lists, which change dynamically and without restrictions.

A LISP system generally includes more than just the interpreter for the LISP language. It consists of several convenient modules to support the development and supervision of programs, e.g., editor, file system, trace function. To increase the execution speed of completed programs, a compiler is generally also available.

Section 5.3 describes how these facilities may be implemented.

5.3   Interlisp-D

Interlisp-D is an interactive LISP programming system which was developed for workstations with graphics facilities, making intensive use of the graphics capabilities.

Interlisp-D comprises the programming language Interlisp, predefined functions, and a programming environment which offers the developer a set of powerful programming tools tailored specifically for the Interlisp-D language.

This system provides an interpreter and a compiler. It supports the programming of parallel processes and a workstation connection to a computer network. A user interface with window features was developed especially for workstations. Almost all to the tools described on the following pages operate in their own windows and are menu-driven using a mouse. The system offers additional support for program development and supervision through the use of the following tools:

- *Structure-oriented Editor*

  The editor can be used to process LISP structures, i.e., functions and data. LISP expressions are monitored during editing to ensure that they conform to the correct list structure.

- *Break Package (Debugger)*

  Using the break package, the user can analyze the status of the system, e.g., have the values of variables output or the call sequence of functions displayed (backtrace). Even during program execution, for example, function calls and current parameter assignments can be traced.

- *Inspector*

  The inspector supports the analysis of complex data structures and selectively modifies specific values in these structures. However, it does not check whether the changes are logical. This is the responsibility of the user.

Expert Systems

Figure 5.1 illustrates an application of the Inspector. With the help of the Inspector, the description of the window entitled "MY WINDOW" is displayed, and below this the description of the "BITMAP" of the window (the BITMAP is the dot-by-dot description of a window). In an Inspector window, it is possible to call the Inspector again, in order to further analyze the data structures:

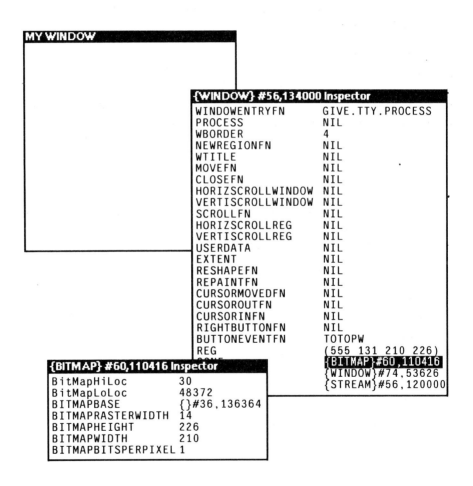

Figure 5.1:   Inspector Application

- *DWIM*

  The "Do What I Mean" package attempts to correct typing errors made by the user.

  Example

76←(Mpcar '(1 2 3) 'MINUS)	User input
= MAPCAR	System output: Correction
(-1 -2 -3)	System output: Result

- *Programmer's Assistant*

  The programmer's assistant makes it possible to enter commands to repeat (with slight changes, if applicable) or cancel previously entered LISP instructions. For this purpose, a list is maintained in which the most recently executed instructions are recorded.

- *Pretty Printer*

  The pretty printer can be used to display functions in a neat form, i.e., with indenting and different print styles.

- *Masterscope*

  The Masterscope can be used to analyze programs, e.g., with regard to function calls or access to variables. For example, the question **"WHO CALLS F"** results in the output of all functions that call the function F.

  The example below illustrates the analysis of the small file TEST, which consists of four functions. (The texts preceded by an arrow "←" are user input. The other texts are system responses.)

  ```
  18←. ANALYZE FUNCTIONS ON 'TEST
  done
  19←. WHO CALLS WHO
  FUN2 -- (B)
  FUN -- (A B FUN2)
  done
  20←. SHOW PATHS FROM FUN
  ```

```
1. FUN   A
2.        B
3.        FUN2  B
NIL
21←. WHO USES X LOCALLY
(FUN)
22←. WHO USES Y LOCALLY
NIL
```

Function FUN calls functions A, B, and FUN2; FUN2 calls B. X is used as a local variable by function FUN; Y, on the other hand, is not used as a local variable by any function.

- *Record/Data Type Package*

  This package allows the user to define records and user data structures.

- *File Package*

  The file package provides support for the user when saving functions and data. For example, the system saves only those functions which have actually been modified, and, upon request indicates to the user any functions or data which have not yet been assigned to a file.

- *Performance Analysis*

  Performance analysis makes it possible to perform statistical analysis of program runs.

Another form of support offered to the user is CLISP (Conversational LISP), an extension of LISP, which makes available constructs such as **if ... then ... else, for,** and **while**.

The user can also create his own tools, i.e., functions which are then always available, just like the predefined functions. This process is simplified in that LISP does not distinguish between programs and data. As a result, the boundary between the programming environment and the user-defined programs is not strictly defined. The tools are LISP functions which handle programs as data, e.g., the function **COMPILE** (compiler) or **EVAL** (interpreter). There is no operating system level for the users of this programming environment. Functions which are accessible as operating-system functions in other systems are fully integrated in the Interlisp-D environment. The user never has to leave this environment during his work session.

This support offered to the user by Interlisp-D greatly simplifies program development. The programming environments of most modern LISP systems offer features similar to those of Interlisp-D.

6 Shells

This chapter introduces several shells which simplify the development of expert systems for specific applications. The term "shell" is used in a broad sense here: it also includes programming environments and other aids. This extension of the term's definition serves to distinguish shells from the software which is generally understood by the term "tool."

The first shells came into being when, after the creation of an expert system, all information specific to the particular application for which the system was written was extracted, leaving a "shell," i.e., the hull or framework of the expert system.
These remaining functions were the starting point for designing an application-independent shell. A classic example of this process is the EMYCIN shell, which was based on the expert system MYCIN. Since 1980, more and more systems are being developed which are designed purely as shells.

Shells support the development of expert systems. To the knowledge engineer, a shell offers aids such as knowledge representation structures, an inference mechanism, and support for an explanation component.

Often, control structures are also predefined, which make it possible to control knowledge processing. In many cases, the inference mechanism and control structures cannot be clearly separated.
Not all of these components are implemented in the shells which are currently available.

The following are desirable components of a shell:

- A mechanism for formal knowledge representation;

- Tools for structuring the knowledge base;

- An inference mechanism;

- A user interface suitable for creating an expert system, building and expanding the knowledge base, and for the end users;

- Support for the creation of an explanation component;

- Mechanisms for consistency checks, troubleshooting and knowledge base expansion;

- Tools for knowledge acquisition.

A shell, therefore, consists of those parts of an expert system that are independent of the expert's knowledge. With a powerful shell, the developer can concentrate entirely on building the knowledge base. Thus, the use of shells reduces the development effort for expert systems. Another advantage in using shells is that they require no profound knowledge of the underlying language.

However, these advantages are counteracted by a series of disadvantages:

- Despite all the flexibility these shells may offer, the developer is bound to the basic concept of the shell. A specific shell cannot form the basis for just any expert system; rather, it is suitable only for specific applications (e.g., diagnosis).

- The developer must learn the language and systematics of the shell selected. This curtails the advantage cited above, that no profound knowledge of the underlying programming language is required.

- Adding new functions, or modifying existing ones, is possible only with shells that provide an interface to a programming language. This option, however, requires more extensive knowledge of the languages involved, thereby defeating the above-mentioned advantage of shorter training times.
  Unfortunately, the implementation of supplementary functions often cannot be avoided, even if the most suitable shell has been selected. Furthermore, the design of the user interface is seldom flexible enough to cover the requirements of all end users.

- The use of shells is restricted because prices are still high and the shells can operate on only a few computers.

In spite of these disadvantages, the use of a shell is advisable, at least initially, in order to speed up the creation of an expert system and to create a demo model.

Most shells are designed for LISP systems because LISP, unlike PROLOG with its backtracking, does not have its own inference mechanism.

The selection of shells ranges from the very simple, providing support only for knowledge representation, to the very complex, providing several forms of knowledge representation as well as a number of different inference strategies.

Of course the scope, and hence the power, of a shell also depends on the hardware used: PC, workstation, mainframe, etc.

Some powerful shells are available only on special workstations. Others can also run, in reduced form, on a PC -- either as a development environment, or as a run-time version (delivery system) of a completed expert system.

The sections that follow describe several shells having various ranges of capabilities.

6.1 The S.1 Shell

The S.1 shell is offered in two variants: a development system for development of and consultation with expert systems, and a run-time system only for consultation with expert systems (that were created with the S.1 development system). An important distinction between the development system and the run-time system of S.1 is that the latter is used without the explanation and acquisition components of the development system.

S.1 was originally based on LISP. Since then, S.1 applications have primarily been based on the C language.

Siemens markets S.1 for APS 58xx (LISP basis) and for SINIX and BS2000 computers (C basis).

The main areas of application for S.1 are diagnosis, recommendation, and classification (e.g., error diagnosis; recommendations for repair work; assigning problem descriptions to predefined problem classes). Objects in the problem area and their properties are described by means of classes and their attributes. Backward-chaining rules determine the values of attributes, taking certainty factors into consideration. Control blocks represent procedural knowledge and control the sequence of a consultation, i.e., which attributes are to be determined, and when (see Chapter 5). A depiction of the user interface and a summary will conclude the description of S.1.

6.1.1 Classes

Classes describe the objects of a problem area for which S.1 is to collect information and make inferences. In contrast to other shells, in S.1 the properties of elements in classes are not represented in the slots of the class, but rather in *attributes* which must be defined separately. Rules and attributes operate on the *instances* of classes. During a consultation, instances can be created dynamically for each class. Conceptually, classes and their instances essentially correspond to the class units and member units in the KEE system (see Section 6.2).

The definiton of a class must specify how many instances of the class may be created during a consultation.

Example

```
DEFINE    CLASS    CAR
       ::  NUMBER.INSTANCES      1
       ::  PRINT.ID            "car #"
```

In this case, the **Number.Instances** slot specifies that exactly one instance of the class "CAR" must be created during a consultation. This instance is given the name "car 1". Instead of a simple number in the "number of instances" slot, one of the instructions **any, at.least number, at.most number** could have been used. In the case of **any,** an arbitrary number of instances may be created; for **at.least number,** a minimum of **number** instances must be created; for **at.most number**, a maximum of **number** instances may be created.

Number.Instances is the only slot of a class definiton that must always be filled in. Most of the other optional slots control the communication with the user of the expert system:

For example, several syntactical variants of the class name may be specified, which S.1 uses when automatically generating quasi-natural-language output. The corresponding grammatical functions, of course, are based on the English language and are not suitable for German, for example.

Instances of a class are generated by

– an instruction in a control block (see Section 6.1.4)

– a reference in the premise part of a rule to an instance which has not yet been created (see Section 6.1.3).

6.1.2 Attributes, Class Hierarchies

Attributes represent the information acquired by an expert system during consultation, whether by applying rules or by asking questions of the user. Definiton of an attribute requires the specification of a name, the names of the classes for which is is applicable, and any restrictions on the values which it can assume.

Example

```
DEFINE    ATTRIBUTE    symptom
       :: DEFINED.ON   CAR
       :: TYPE         text
```

The attribute "symptom" applies to instances of the class "CAR" and can store values of the type **text**, e.g., symptom (car 1) = car.doesnt.start.

There are four value ranges for an attribute: **text, integer, real** and **Boolean. Integer** and **real** attributes store numbers (e.g., maximum speed, mileage rating); Boolean attributes are either **true** or **false;** e.g., "new.car" - yes or no.

If necessary, the value range of an attribute can be further restricted by means of the **Legal.Values** slot.

Example

```
:: LEGAL.VALUES      {car.doesnt.start
                      weak.or.flickering.light,
                      other.symptoms}
```

In the example, only three values are legal for the attribute "symptom" (toward the end of this S.1 description, the individual examples of classes, attributes, rules, and control blocks are combined in a small expert system, which assigns the symptoms of a defective car to a type of fault).

As mentioned earlier, the value of an attribute is determined during consultation by applying rules or by asking questions of the user. The **Legal.Means** slot can be used to specify whether one of these two options for the attribute is to be ruled out.

Example

```
:: LEGAL.MEANS     {query.user}   In this case, only queries to
                                   the user are allowed.
Otherwise:         {try.rules}
```

The question which is to be asked in order to determine the attribute value is enterd in the **Prompt** slot.

Example

```
:: PROMPT    "What is wrong with"  !
             instance.trans(CAR)! "?"
```

Instance.trans is a function which supplies the name of the corresponding instance of the class. The exclamation point "!" is used to concatenate two strings.

A defective car may exhibit several symptoms at the same time. Therefore, it is sensible to store several values in the attribute "symptom." The slot which defines whether an attribute may have only one value, or any number of values, is called the **Multivalued** slot.

Example

```
:: MULTIVALUED  true
```

Consequently, more than one value is allowed for the attribute "symptom," i.e., in response to the question "What is wrong with car 1?" the user can enter, for example, "car.doesnt.start" and "other.symptoms."

The complete definition of "symptom" is now as follows:

Example

```
DEFINE   ATTRIBUTE       symptom
      :: DEFINED.ON      CAR
      :: TYPE            text
      :: MULTIVALUED     true
      :: LEGAL.VALUES    {car.doesnt.start,
                         weak.or.flickering.light,
                         other.symptoms}
      :: LEGAL.MEANS     {query.user}
      :: PROMPT          "What is wrong with" !
                         instance.trans (CAR)
                         ! "?"
END.DEFINE
```

Another attribute that will be needed later is "is.defective":

Example

```
DEFINE   ATTRIBUTE       is.defective
      :: DEFINED.ON      CAR
      :: TYPE            text
      :: MULTIVALUED     false
      :: LEGAL.VALUES    {mechanical.system,
                         electrical.system,
                         tank.empty}
      :: LEGAL.MEANS     {try.rules}
      :: POST.DETERMINATION.BLOCK   fault.area
END.DEFINE
```

Section 6.1.3 describes three rules which assign fault types to specific combinations of symptoms.

An important feature of S.1 has not yet been discussed: the processing of "certainty factors." S.1 makes it possible to assign a number between <-1> and <1> to the information contained in an attribute. This number is called the certainty factor, or confidence factor. It is not equivalent to the confidence factors as used in probability and statistics. $<-1>$ means "absolutely false"; $<1>$ means "absolutely true."

If the user is asked for the value of an attribute which may assume only one value (::MULTIVALUED false), he can still specify several values, provided that he states a certainty factor for each value.

In this case, the attribute values with different certainty factors represent conflicting hypotheses with regard to the actual value. However, as soon as one of the values receives the factor $<1>$, it becomes certain, and the conflicting values can be cancelled.

The backward-chaining rules of S.1 also take into consideration the certainty factors of the attribute values and modify them where applicable (see Chapter 4).

When S.1 has exhausted all the valid options ("legal.means" slot) for calculating the value of an attribute for an instance, then this value can no longer be modified, i.e., it is "fixed", along with its certainty factor. The same is true when an attribute value receives the certainty factor $<1>$ in the course of the consultation: from this moment on, the value can no longer be modified for the remainder of the consultation.

For example, if a user answers "car.doesnt.start" in response to the question regarding the symptoms of the defective car, then the attribute "symptom" is assigned this value with the certainty factor $<1>$ for the instance "car 1," because no certainty factor was stated explicitly. From this point on, the value "car.doesnt.start" can no longer be modified, not even by applying rules or by asking the user additional questions.

With multivalued attributes, the processing of certainty factors is less complicated: the various attribute values for an instance are mutually independent and may all have the certainty factor $<1>$, for example.

As with other tools, class hierarchies may also be set up in S.1. For this purpose, "Class Types" must be defined, which include a **contains** slot, in which the subordinate class types and classes are entered.

Example

```
DEFINE   CLASS.TYPE     SHIP
         :: CONTAINS     {sailing.ship, steamship}
END.DEFINE
```

"sailing.ship" and "steamship" are either simple classes or class types, which in turn may contain additional classes or class types.

In the **defined.on** slot of an attribute, the name of a class type may be specified, so that the attribute is valid for all instances of the classes contained in the class type. For example, the attribute "maximum speed" applies not only to cars, but to all means of locomotion.

6.1.3 Rules

The rules in S.1, like most rules, have a **premise** and a **conclusion**. The conclusion of an S.1 rule serves to determine attribute values or to modify their certainty factors. The premise part is generally used for checking attribute values.

Example

```
DEFINE  RULE           RULE.1
        ::APPLIED.TO    a: CAR
        ::PREMISE       symptom [a] is car.doesnt.start
        ::CONCLUSION    is.defective [a] = tank.empty <0.9>
END.DEFINE
```

RULE.1 is applied to instances of the class CAR, where the name of the instance is linked to the variable **a.** The premise of RULE.1 checks whether the attribute **symptom** has the value **car.doesnt.start** for **a.** If so, **is.defective** for **a** receives the value **tank.empty.**

When a rule is processed, certainty factors must be taken into consideration in three places:

a) The attribute values in the premise have a certainty factor which is less than <1>:
S.1 calculates a combined certainty factor for the entire premise, based on the certainty factors of the individual attribute values. If the combined certainty factor is greater than <0.2>, the rule may be applied.

b) The conclusion of the rule is supplied with a certainty factor (<0.9> in the example):
The "conclusion certainty factor" is valid if the premise is true. If not, then S.1 calculates the product of the combined certainty factor and the conclusion certainty factor, and enters the attribute value with this "overall certainty factor" into the knowledge base.

c) The attribute value in the conclusion is already present in the knowledge base with a certainty factor (e.g., if several rules calculate the same attribute value):

In this case, S.1 generates a new certainty factor from the overall certainty factor for the rule and the existing certainty factor of the attribute value. This is done by means of a formula developed for MYCIN, one of the first expert systems: Let x and y be the two certainty factors to be combined, and CF-Combine the calculating function. Then:

$$
\text{CF-Combine}(x,y) =
\begin{cases}
1 > x, y > 0 : x + y - (x{*}y) \\
-1 < x, y < 0 : x + y + (x{*}y) \\
\left.\begin{array}{l} 0 < x < 1, 0 > y > -1 \\ \text{or} \\ 0 > x > -1, 0 < y < 1 \end{array}\right\} : \dfrac{x + y}{1 - \min(|x|,|y|)}
\end{cases}
$$

Example   1-min (|x|, |y|)

Let us assume that the user has responded to the question regarding the symptoms of his defective car with "car.doesnt.start <0.8>", and the value of "is.defective[car 1]" has already been determined from other rules as "tank.empty <0.5>."

S.1 first attempts to apply RULE.1:
The rule has only one premise, so the combined certainty factor is <0.8> and RULE.1 can fire. The overall certainty factor for the

rule is calculated as $<0.72>$ ($= <0.8> * <0.9>$). The CF-Combine function is then applied to determine the new certainty factor for "is. defective [car 1] = car.doesnt.start":

CF-Combine (0.72, 0.5) = 0.86

Thus, by applying RULE.1, the certainty factor of the attribute value has been modified to $<0.86>$.

S.1 allows several attributes to be specified in the conclusion of a rule and/or several values to be specified for one attribute.

Example

```
DEFINE RULE          RULE.2
       ::APPLIED.TO   a: CAR
       ::PREMISE      symptom [a] is
       weak.or.flickering.light
       ::CONCLUSION   is.defective[a] = electrical.system
                                       <0.9>
                                       tank.empty <-0.5>
END DEFINE

DEFINE RULE          RULE.3
       ::APPLIED.TO   a: CAR
       ::PREMISE      symptom[a] is other.symptoms
       ::CONCLUSION   is.defective[a] = mechanical.system
                                       <0.9>,
                                       electrical.system
                                       <-0.5>,
                                       tank.empty <-0.5>
END DEFINE
```

Even though "is.defective" was defined as "single valued" (i.e., ::MULTIVALUED false), RULE.2 and RULE.3 can assign several values to the attribute - each provided with a certainty factor - which function, as it were, as conflicting hypotheses for the "true" value of the attribute.

Of course, there may also be more than one attribute in the premise of an S.1 rule. In this case, a test is generally performed to determine whether the certainty factor of the attribute value (for a specific instance) lies within a given range. For the premise "symptom[a] is car. doesnt.start," the keyword "is" means, for example, that the value of "symptom[a]" to be tested must have a certainty factor greater than $<0.2>$. If "definitely.is" had been used instead of "is," then the certainty factor would have had to be $<1>$.

If the certainty factor lies within the predefined range, then the test is successfully completed and the tested attribute is replaced by its certainty factor; otherwise, it is replaced by "false" (i.e., $<-1>$). This is necessary because several attribute tests can be linked by means of operators similar to those used in predicate logic, and a combined certainty factor must be calculated for the rule premise (as mentioned earlier, a rule fires only if the combined certainty factor is greater than $<0.2>$). Suppose, for example, that "test1 and test2" is the somewhat simplified premise of a rule. The combined certainty factor for this premise is equal to the minimum of the certainty factors of {test1, test2}. The certainty factor of "test1 or test2" is equal to the maximum of the certainty factors of {test1, test2}. The certainty factor of "not test" is $<-1>$; if "test" is successful, the certainty factor is $<1>$.

Example

Suppose the user has entered the values "car.doesnt.start $<0.5>$" and "other symptoms $<0.9>$" for "symptom[car 1]," and that there is a rule with the following premise:

(not (symptom[a] definitely.is other.symptoms)
and (symptom[a] is car.doesnt.start)).

Since "definitely.is" requires a certainty factor $= <1>$, which "other.symptoms" does not possess, the first test within the "not" clause fails and is replaced by $<-1>$. The second test within the "and" clause is successful, so the premise now has the following form:

(not ($<-1>$) and ($<0.5>$))
$= (<1>)$ and ($<0.5>$) $= <0.5>$

Therefore, the premise has a combined certainty factor of $<0.5>$.

In addition to the operators **and, or,** and **not,** S.1 provides quantifiers with which the value for an attribute can be tested for several instances of a class:

- **for.all declaration test** performs the "test" for all instances of the classes specified in the "declaration." If there are fewer instances than the number allowed in the "number.instances" slot of a class, the missing instances are created automatically. If the "for.all" test is successful, it returns the smallest certainty factor found in testing the instances.

- **for.all.existing declaration test** is equivalent to "for.all", with the added restriction that no new instances are created.

- **exists declaration** causes S.1 to search for an instance which satisfies the restrictions specified in the declaration. If such an instance exists, the "exists" expression returns the certainty factor of the restriction.

- **try.each declaration** makes it possible to have the same rule fire several times. If the premise of the rule consists of only the "try.each" expression, then the rule fires exactly once for each instance that satisfies the restrictions in the declaration.

Unfortunately, space limitations do not permit a more detailed discussion of the quantifiers listed above, which is not to say, however, that the quantifiers are unimportant. On the contrary, they represent a significant improvement in the "power" of rules, as compared to tools which recognize only the operators **and, or,** and **not** for the conditions of a rule.

To reiterate, S.1 rules are used to calculate the certainty factors for attribute values. In doing this, S.1 follows a backward-chaining strategy:

In a control block, S.1 receives the instruction to determine the value of attribute A1. Rules can then be applied whose conclusions contain A1. It is possible, however, that the premises of these rules contain the attributes $A_2 \ldots A_n$, whose values are not yet known, so that $A_2 \ldots A_n$ must first be calculated using other rules, and so on. If the calculation of an attribute value by means of rules fails, the user can be asked for the value, provided that this is permitted based on the **legal.means** slot of the attribute.

6.1.4 Control blocks

Consultations in S.1 are controlled by so-called "control blocks," which are written in a procedural programming language, the "S.1 Knowledge Base Language."

Control blocks define when and which attributes are to be determined, and when and which messages are to be printed out for the user. Every knowledge base needs a control block, whose **invocation** slot has the value **top.level**. This top level control block is automatically executed when the user starts the expert system, and thus serves as the "framework" in which the consultation takes place. The consultation ends as soon as the processing of the top-level control block has been completed.

Example

```
DEFINE   CONTROL.BLOCK    CAR.FAULT.LOCATION
::  INVOCATION    top.level
::  BODY     begin
                 vars  a: CAR;
                 create.instance  CAR      called a:
                 determine symptom [a];
                 determine is.defective [a]
             end
END.DEFINE
```

This control block first creates an instance of the class "CAR", and links its name to the variable "a". The values of the attributes "symptom" and "is.defective" are then calculated for the instance, and the consultation is ended.

A control block can call other control blocks (as "subroutines" or "procedures"), and variables can be transferred to them. The **invocation** slot of the called control blocks must have the value **internal**.
Two additional types of control blocks facilitate a limited forward-chaining strategy during rule processing:

- If the **invocation** slot has the value **post.instantiation**, the control block is always executed when an instance of a class has been created whose **post.instantiation.block** slot contains the name of the control block.

– **post.determination** control blocks are executed as soon as the value of a specific attribute has been determined for an instance.

Example

```
DEFINE   CONTROL.BLOCK    FAULT.AREA
:: ARGUMENTS      is.defective:attributes
                  a: CAR

:: BODY    begin
             if is.defective [a] is tank.empty
                then display "Please check whether the tank is
                empty. "! newline ( );
             if is.defective [a] is electrical.system
                then display "The fault is probably in the
                electrical system. "! newline ( );
             if is.defective [a] is mechanical.system
                then display "The fault is probably in the
                mechanical system. "! newline ( )
           end
END.DEFINE
```

After the value of "is.defective [car 1]" has been determined, "fault.area" is executed and displays a recommendation for the user.

post.determination control blocks represent an element of forward inferencing when they include **determine** instructions, for example, which make it necessary to determine the values of other attributes. These attributes, in turn, may have their own **post.determination** control blocks. The determination of an attribute value thus triggers a search for the values of other attributes, and so on.

Aside from this rather complicated forward mechanism, however, **post.instantiation** and **post.determination** control blocks represent, above all, a convenient way to keep the user informed about the current status of a consultation.

6.1.5 User Interface

The user interface of the S.1 shell (development system) is available in a graphics as well as a non-graphics version. The graphics-based user interface of S.1 is comparable in convenience to other shells in the higher price range (e.g., KEE, ART). The execution of a consultation can be represented in graphic form in this shell. An extensive mouse-activated menu system simplifies the use of the tool and can be used for entering new data interactively or modifying classes, attributes, rules, and control blocks. The "Typescript Window" is used for interaction with the user. Figure 6.1 shows an S.1 screen after execution of a consultation with the expert system used in our example:

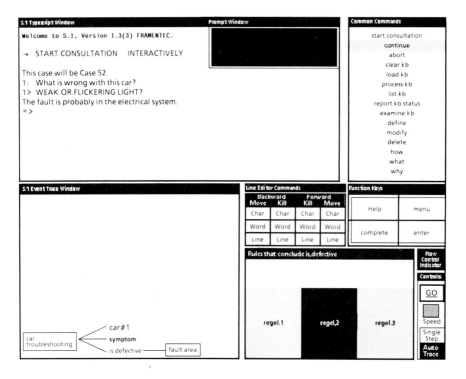

Figure 6.1:   S.1 Screen After a Consultation

The typescript window shows the expert system's question ("What is wrong with this car?"), the user's answer, and the response from the system. By clicking the mouse on the "menu" field, the user can be shown his response options (as defined in the "legal.values" slot of the attribute) to a question from the system.

The classes, control blocks, and attributes used during the consultation are displayed in the Event Trace Window. Another window shows which rules were checked and which rules could fire.

6.1.6 Summary

S.1 is a user-friendly tool for creating diagnostic expert systems, particularly when uncertain knowledge must be processed. In this respect, S.1 follows in the tradition of EMYCIN, but it also features several important improvements: premises of rules can be combined by means of powerful operators; control blocks allow for precise control of the consultation; classes or instances represent objects of the problem area.

S.1 has some limitations, though, which make it unsuitable for some problem areas:
In principle, rules are processed backwards; there is no inheritance mechanism for classes and superclasses, and attribute values are determined only once, after which they can no longer be modified. This last point is likely to be a serious handicap, especially in those applications where time factors must be taken into consideration.

6.2 The KEE Shell

The KEE (Knowledge Engineering Environment) shell is an expert
system shell which ranks among the most advanced and comprehensive
shells currently available for commercial applications. Accordingly,
KEE requires powerful hardware (XEROX 11xx, SIEMENS APS 58xx,
SYMBOLICS, TI Explorer) and lies in the high-price range. In the KEE
shell, object-oriented and rule-based knowledge representation forms
can be combined. For this reason, shells like KEE are called "hybrid
shells." Furthermore, it is possible to code procedural knowledge directly in LISP.

6.2.1 Object-Oriented Knowledge Representation

The basic unit of knowledge representation is the object, called a "unit"
in KEE. All items, concepts, and abstractions of a problem area are represented as units in KEE. Rules, too, represent nothing more than special units. Each unit has an arbitrary number of "slots," in which the attributes of the unit are described. Each slot represents one attribute of
the unit and has several "facets," in which the attribute is specified in
more detail.

The unit "My car" could have a slot with the name "Color" and the facet
"Value: Red." The value of a slot is stored in one of its facets. In the
example, "My car" has the attribute with the name "Color" and the
value "Red."

A slot also contains other facets which can be used to specify, for example, the value range for the slot value, or whether multiple values are permitted. The number of possible values in a slot is called "Cardinality";
the facet "Cardinality min" specifies the lower limit, "Cardinality max"
the upper limit, for the number of values a slot may have.

Example

The value range for "color" could be defined as (blue, red, green, black, white); for multicolored cars, the "color" slot must hold multiple values. It would then make sense to assign "Cardinality min" the value 1, and "Cardinality max" the value 5; i.e., the car may have between one and five different colors. The experienced KEE user can change the predefined facets and also define completely new facets. The figure below illustrates the relationships between unit, slots, and facets:

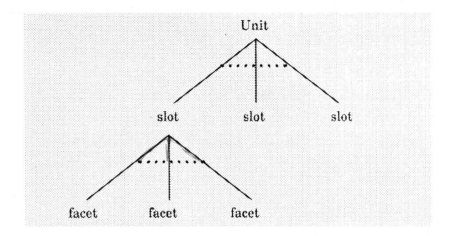

In the example,

```
Unit:   Car
Slot:   Color
    Facet Value              value "red"
    Facet Comment            value "Color is an attribute of the unit
                             car"
    Facet Value Class        value one of {blue, red, green, black,
                             white}
    Facet Cardinality min    value 1
    Facet Cardinality max    value 5
Slot:                            :

                                 :

    .

    .

    .
```

All facets have a name and a value, but the facet with the name "Value" stores the value of the slot. The other facets have as their values the specifications for the value of the slot.

There are two types of units: class units and member units.

Member units describe individual objects (e.g., "My car"); class units, on the other hand, group several objects with common attributes into a single class (e.g., "BMWs"). The relationship between a class unit and its associated member units is expressed as follows: The member units are "instances" of the class unit. In other words, they are specific examples of the general concepts expressed by class units. Class units can be arranged in a hierarchy, i.e., one class can be defined as a subclass or superclass of another.

Example

"Cars" is the superclass of "BMWs," and "My car" is an instance of the class "BMWs" (provided my car is a BMW).

In the diagram below, the links between classes and subclasses are represented by solid lines, and the links between classes and instances (member units) by broken lines.

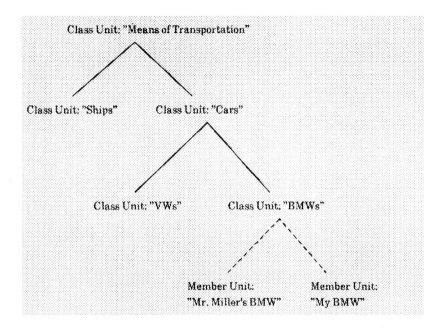

The arrangement of classes in a hierarchy, in which the more abstract and comprehensive classes are the superclasses of more narrowly defined classes, is important for the mechanism called "inheritance." Inheritance means that the slots in a class unit are automatically copied to its subordinate class and member units (this refers only to the inheritance of empty slots, i.e., slots without values. The inheritance of slot values will be discussed later). Thus, a knowledge base can be built more effectively when several objects in a problem area have the same attributes. For example, *all* cars in active use definitely possess the attribute "mileage rating," expressed in miles per gallon. The "mileage rating" slot needs to be defined only once in the class units "car" and is then automatically available in all subclasses and in all instances of the class "cars" and its subclasses.

On the other hand, there is no point in inheriting an attribute which is valid only for the class unit for which it was defined. An example of such an attribute would be "Price of the least expensive model" for the class "BMWs." The inheritance of this slot by subclasses or instances is prevented in KEE by designating it is an "Own Slot." In contrast, inheritable slots are called "Member Slots." A member unit, of course, possesses only own slots, since member units, by definition, cannot have subclasses or instances.

In KEE, not only slots may be inherited, but also slot values. If the class "Vehicles" has the attribute "Number of wheels," and if this member slot has the value "2" in the subclass "Motorcycles," then this value can also be transferred to all instances of the subclass. The knowledge engineer can control the inheritance of slot values in many ways by utilizing the "Inheritance Role" facet of a unit. The default setting of this facet is "Override Values," which means that a special slot value determined for the unit under consideration supersedes the inherited slot value (in the example above, the class unit "Uncommon Motorcycles," a subclass of "Motorcycles," the value "3" is assigned to the slot "Number of wheels"; "3" then supersedes the previously inherited "2").

Inheritance, therefore, is determined by two factors:

– A slot must be defined as a member slot so that it can be inherited.

– Whether and how the value of a slot is inherited depends on its inheritance role facet.

As soon as a unit is created, it automatically receives all member slots of its superordinate units, regardless of whether these slots have values assigned to them.

In some cases, it is desirable for a class to have two mutually independent superclasses:

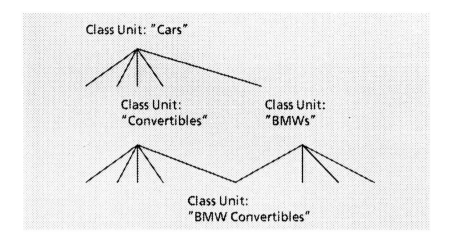

In this case, the class "BMW Convertibles" inherits the slots of both superclasses. This inheritance mechanism is called "Multiple Inheritance" and is a valuable aid in merging two different concepts ("Herbivorous life-forms" + "Humans" = "Vegetarians").

6.2.2 Rule-Based Knowledge Representation

The previous section describes how KEE could be used to represent and organize the individual items in a specific problem area. What is still missing, however, is an inferencing or planning process based on the units, i.e., the integration of rule-based knowledge.

Rules have the following format in KEE:

(IF <condition>

THEN <conclusion> <conclusion> . . .

DO <action> <action> . . .)

Actions are arbitrary LISP expressions that can be evaluated. Conclusions are expressed in a so-called TellAndAsk language, which can be used to query and modify the knowledge base. Conditions are either LISP or TellAndAsk expressions. When the conditions are satisfied, the conclusions and actions are implemented.

First, a few explanations regarding the TellAndAsk language:

A typical expression reads as follows:

(ASSERT '(MY.CAR IS IN BMW)),

whereby the knowledge base is informed that MY CAR is an instance of the class BMWs.
Class/subclass links are generated as follows:

(ASSERT '(ALL MERCEDES ARE CARS))

Three other important TellAndAsk commands are **QUERY, ASK.USER,** and **RETRACT**.

QUERY searches the knowledge base for facts;
For example, (QUERY '(ALL ?Z ARE CARS) 'ALL) outputs all the subclasses of the class CARS. ?Z is a variable which, in this case, represents the subclasses of CARS and which is to be assigned all the existing values by KEE. Variables are characterized by a question mark preceding their name.

ASK.USER poses questions to the user, and the answers are entered directly in the knowledge base. For example, when the expression

(ASK.USER (?X IS IN PUMPS)) is processed, the expert system asks the user

What is in class PUMPS?

RETRACT removes arbitrary slot values and class/subclass or class/member relations from the knowledge base.

TellAndAsk expressions can be nested and linked with "and," "or," "not," and "equal."

The commands described above are intended mainly for conclusions, to transfer to the knowledge base the new information gained through the application of a rule. In conditions, simple TellAndAsk expressions are used (without commands), which can be either true or false and which, in effect, must be understood as assertions:

```
(IF     ((MY.CAR IS IN CLASS CARS)
        AND (THE COLOR OF MY.CAR IS RED))
THEN    (MY.CAR IS IN CLASS RED.CARS))
```

Since rules in KEE are nothing more than member units, the rules can also be grouped by means of class formation. Thus, it is possible to segment the rule base of a large expert system, and activate only that group of rules which is needed at the moment. This increases the speed of execution for the expert system and helps to keep knowledge bases, even large ones, manageable.

All rules in KEE can be evaluated via forward chaining as well as backward chaining.

Forward chaining can be initiated in two ways:

-- An ASSERT command is entered, either in a rule or directly by the user, which contains the name of a rule class; the expert system then attempts to determine all the implications of the new information by applying all the rules in the specified rule class.

- A class of "active assert rules" is assigned to a slot; the rules are then activated automatically as soon as the slot changes its value.

Backward chaining is initiated by a QUERY command, which - like ASSERT - must contain the name of a rule class. The TellAndAsk expression within the QUERY command normally contains one or more variables for which the backward chainer is to search for values (see the above example of the QUERY command). The expert system first searches its knowledge base to determine whether the corresponding values already exist (i.e., whether there are values for which the TellAndAsk expression in the QUERY command is known to be true). If this is not the case, the rules of the specified rule class are applied. If this is unsuccessful as well, the values for the variables can then be requested from the user.

6.2.3 Example of a Knowledge Base

Having shown how object-oriented and rule-based knowledge can be represented in KEE, we can now build a small but functional knowledge base. The purpose of the sample expert system is to make recommendations to the user regarding the purchase of a car, and to ask him appropriate questions about his requirements.

First, the objects of the problem area must be represented as KEE units. There are several types of cars which may be considered by the buyer:

BMW 520, BMW 520td, SAAB d, VW Golf, VW Golf D, Renault 5, Renault 5 GLD.

Each car type represents a seperate class unit (not a member unit). The car types can be arranged according to manufacturer; the result is shown n Figure 6.2.

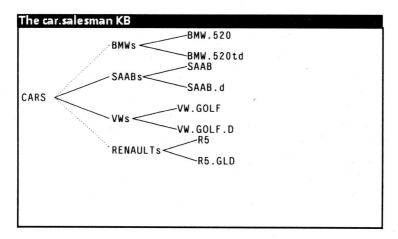

Figure 6.2: Example of a Class Unit

Also required is a member unit which represents the desired car, and which is first created as an instance of the class "Cars." This member unit, called "desired.car" for the sake of simplicity, is assigned as an instance of the desired car class as the result of the expert system consultation.

The cars can now be supplied with attributes by assigning slots to the class unit "Cars":

"Engine,"   with the permissible values {diesel, gasoline}
"Price,"   with the permissible values {expensive, inexpensive}
"Origin,"   with the permissible values {German, foreign}

These slots are automatically inherited by all subclasses of "Cars" and also by the instance "desired.car," and must now be supplied with the corresponding values. For the Renault 5 GLD, the values are, for example:

Engine: diesel, Price: inexpensive, Origin: foreign

The slots of "desired.car" remain empty for the time being, since the user of the expert system must be asked for the values of these slots.

Finally, some rules must be defined which assign a specific combination of attributes (customer's requirements) to the corresponding type of car.

Two such rules are, for example:

(BMW.RULE	(IF	((The origin OF desired.car IS German)
		AND
		(THE price OF desired.car IS expensive))
	THEN	(desired.car IS IN CLASS BMWs)))
(BMW.520td.RULE	(IF	((desired.car IS IN CLASS BMWs)
		AND
		(THE engine OF desired.car IS diesel))
	THEN	(desired.car IS IN CLASS BMW.520td)))

The rules for the BMW.520 and the other three makes of cars (six cars in all) are formulated in the same way. The result is a total of 12 rules.

The expert system is now complete. In order to assign the desired car to a specific class, the user can then ask the system the following question, for example:

(QUERY '(desired.car IS IN CLASS ?WHICH) 'ALL CAR.RULES)

With 'ALL, the expert system is instructed to find all possible values of the variable ?WHICH; 'CAR.RULES is the name of the rule class to be used for backward chaining.

During the processing of this query, the user is asked questions about the engine, price, and origin. Figures 6.3 and 6.4 show the difference in the assignment of "desired.car" to the classes before and after the consultation. Figure 6.5 illustrates the result unit "desired.car" after the consultation.

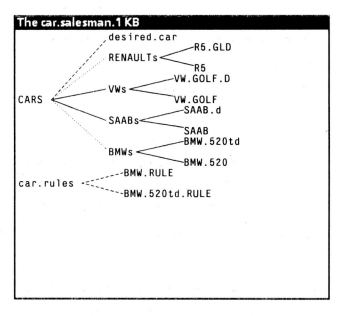

Figure 6.3: Before Consultation

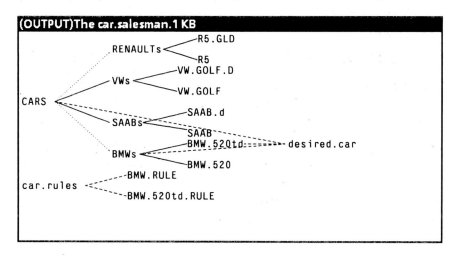

Figure 6.4: After Consultation

```
┌──────────────────────────────────────────────────┐
│ (OUTPUT) The desired.car unit                      │
├──────────────────────────────────────────────────┤
│ Unit:desired.car in knowledge base                 │
│ car.salesman.1                                     │
│ Created by on 27-Mar-86 13:25:06                   │
│ Modified by KURT on 27-Mar-86 14:08:43            │
│  Member of:CARS                                    │
│ ──────────────────────────────────────────────    │
│ OwnSlot: ORIGIN from desired.car                   │
│    Inheritance: OVERRIDE.VALUES                     │
│    ValueClass: (ONE.OF German foreign)             │
│    Cardinality.Min: 1                              │
│    Cardinality.Max: 1                              │
│    Values: German                                  │
│                                                    │
│ OwnSlot: ENGINE from desired.car                   │
│    Inheritance: OVERRIDE.VALUES                     │
│    ValueClass: (ONE.OF diesel gasoline)           │
│    Cardinality.Min: 1                              │
│    Cardinality.Max: 1                              │
│    Values:diesel                                   │
│                                                    │
│ OwnSlot: PRICE from desired.car                    │
│    Inheritance: OVERRIDE.VALUES                     │
│    ValueClass: (ONE.OF expensive inexpensive)     │
│    Cardinality.Min: 1                              │
│    Cardinality.Max: 1                              │
│    Values:expansive                               │
│                                                    │
└──────────────────────────────────────────────────┘
```

Figure 6.5:   The Member Unit "desired.car"

It is easy to see that this expert system has a serious disadvantage: it requires 12 rules to process a simple decision tree. This effort can be greatly reduced by fully exploiting the capabilities of KEE, in which case there will be only two rules (Figure 6.6):

Rule 1: (IF (THE STATE OF expert.system IS START)

DO   (ASK.USER '(THE ENGINE OF desired.car IS ?T))
(ASK.USER '(THE ORIGIN OF desired.car IS ?Y))
(ASK.USER '(THE PRICE OF desired.car IS ?Z))
(QUERY' (desired.car IS IN CLASS ?WHICH) 'ALL 'b.rules))

Rule 2: (IF   ((THE ENGINE OF desired.car IS ?T)
AND (THE ENGINE OF ALL ?X IS ?T)
AND (THE PRICE OF desired.car IS ?Z)
AND (THE PRICE OF ALL ?X IS ?Z)
AND (THE ORIGIN OF desired.car IS ?Y)
AND (THE ORIGIN OF ALL ?X IS ?Y))
THEN (desired.car IS IN CLASS ?X))

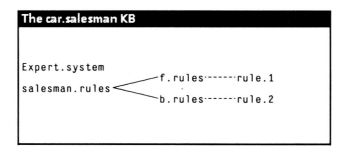

Figure 6.6: The Unit "Expert.system"

"Expert.system" is a new unit with a slot called STATE. The consultation is initiated by assigning the value START to the STATE slot (via ASSERT) and evaluating this new information in the forward direction by means of f.rules. Rule.1 is then executed automatically, asking the user about the engine, price, and origin of the desired car, and then calling rule.2 backward. In rule.2, KEE tries to find values for ?X, ?Y, ?Z, and ?T which satisfy the conditions in the condition part of the rule. (Variables in KEE are always defined locally for a rule.) There is only one possible value each for ?Y, ?Z, and ?T, namely the one entered by the user in rule.1. All eight cars are applicable to ?X, and their slot values can be compared with the values for ?V, ?Z, and ?T.

Of course, both of these rules are only meaningful because it is understood from the start that all slot values (engine, origin, and price) must be queried so that the desired car is clearly assigned to a particular model. If this were not known, then only the more general solution path with the 12 rules would be applicable.

6.2.4 Additional Notes on Knowledge Representation

It was mentioned earlier that procedural knowledge in the form of LISP code can also be integrated into a KEE knowledge base. This is possible in two places:

- Within rules, where LISP expressions that can be evaluated are valid as conditions or actions;

- Within other units via "method slots," which are filled with LISP programs in which TellAndAsk expression are also allowed. The method slots determine how the object responds when a message is received, and the object itself can send messages. Thus, it is possible to control the entire expert system by means of a method slot installed in a special unit (e.g., class unit "Expert system manager"). This method slot, which could be called the top level, supervises the sequence of a consultation by creating and deleting units, initiating rule class execution, and deciding whether the consultation has been completed. To start the expert system, the user simply activates the top-level method slot.

Therefore, knowledge representation in KEE has three components:

- representation of the objects of the problem area through units and slots;

- representation of the heuristics of the problem area through rules;

- representation of the control knowledge (how, what, and when knowledge is applied) through LISP code with TellAndAsk expressions.

6.2.5 User Interface

Thanks to window and mouse technology, working with KEE is relatively simple and efficient. Figure 6.7 illustrates a typical KEE screen.

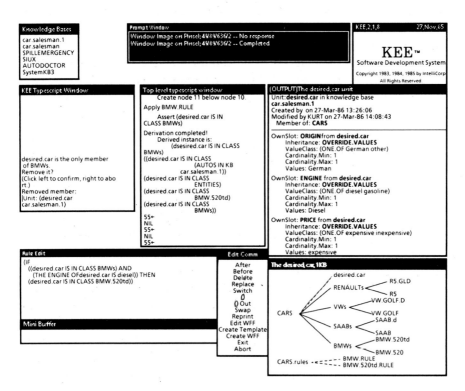

Figure 6.7: The KEE Screen

All commands used in KEE can be entered in two ways:

- By typing them into the Top Level Typescript Window;

- By means of the mouse-activated menus which are provided in the various windows.

The Top Level Typescript Window also allows access to LISP. In the KEE Typescript Window, the system asks for information from the user, e.g., when units and slots are to be created or modified. The Knowledge Bases Window, which is permanently displayed, shows which knowledge bases are available to the user. The Prompt Window reports operating errors and system errors, or provides supplementary information for a menu command which has just been selected. In addition, the user can create any number of KEE windows, so that relevant information can be available on the screen at all times (e.g., structure of the knowledge base, description of individual units, etc.). The user-friendly Interlisp-D editor (DEdit) is available for entering or modifying units (especially rules). As shown in the figures in the previous pages, KEE can represent the knowledge base as a graph, whereby the nodes are units and the connecting links represent class/ subclass or class/instance relationships. The graphical representation provides the user with a good overview of the knowledge base. Individual units can be selected directly by clicking the mouse button and then edited (or deleted or modified in some other way). Since KEE is an interpreting program system, changes in the knowledge base can be tested immediately, using one of several available trace modes. Unfortunately, KEE is very weak in checking the syntactical accuracy of user input, which sometimes causes the LISP interpreter itself to be interrupted by an error. It is usually quite difficult to locate these errors. If, for example, the second argument is left out of a query command - "all" in the previous examples - the LISP system, in some cases, reports the error "non-numeric argument," without any indication of the error location). Particularly a tool as complex as KEE could use syntax checks and perhaps even semantic checks for the entered rules and commands.

Another important feature of KEE is the option of representing slot values in graphic form. For example, if the unit "my.car" has a slot called "speed" with a value range between 0 and 300, then a so-called "active image " with the name "Digiactuator" could be assigned to this slot, which would be permanently displayed on the screen and would indicate the speed of "my.car." Using the mouse, the user could then change the number displayed on the screen, thereby also changing the slot value.

In addition to the relatively simple Digiactuator Image (a rectangle containing a number), there is a whole series of other predefined active images, the appearance of which can also be changed. Thus, the knowledge engineer has the possibility of creating a user interface for his expert system which is particularly well suited for his specific application.

6.2.6 Summary

The concept of knowledge representation in KEE is based on an object-oriented approach using units (also known in other systems as "frames"). Rules are understood to be special units, and control knowledge is incorporated in the rules or in specific slots of units (method slots).

A few words on the possible areas of application for KEE:

Unlike other shells (el.g., MED1, EMYCIN), KEE was not designed exclusively as a diagnostic tool.

There is no predefined construct called "Diagnosis" (see MED1) with an inference mechanism that uses rules and user input exclusively for determining the certainty of diagnoses. KEE is more flexible: Within the specific problem area, the user can ask arbitrary questions, which the expert system attempts to answer with the aid of rules and previously known facts. The user can also actively control a consultation by entering new information and having the expert system determine all the consequences and implications. Theoretically, the concept of object-oriented programming makes it possible to use KEE in the area of process control and process monitoring. Here, it is important to have the option of changing the slot values any number of times during the consultation. For example, a slot called "engine.temperature" can always be kept up-to-date and monitored for critical values. As soon as the engine temperature exceeds the critical value, a class of rules is activated which initiate countermeasures. In practical applications a system used for process control must also meet real-time requirements.

The fact that certainty factors are not standard features of the KEE system should be mentioned. Therefore, when a slot value is entered, it is not possible to include the degree of certainty for the value's validity (for example: The cause of the car's defect is *probably* in the ignition system). The same applies to rules: with KEE, it is not possible to state that conclusions are only "possibly" valid, if the conditions are true (for example: If my car doesn't start, then possibly the tank is empty). In most cases, this problem can be avoided by defining the slots accordingly. In the two examples above, a slot called "possible.causes.of.fault" could be created, in which the values "ignition.system" and "tank.empty" could be entered. The question whether the absence of certainty factors in KEE represents a real shortcoming will have to be considered for each individual application area and expert system project. In any case, the KEE Reference Manual contains instructions on how certainty factors can, in fact, be processed through extensive redefinition and modification of slots.

6.3 The MED1 Shell

The MED1 shell was developed in 1983 at Kaiserslautern University and implemented on several computers. Reference will be made later to the BS2000 version, which runs on Siemens mainframes. The underlying programming language, which cannot be accessed from within MED1, is Interlisp. MED1, as the name implies, is designed specifically for medical diagnostic systems. Due to the specific development objectives (research project), the user interface of MED1 is not nearly as convenient as those in other shells (e.g., KEE, S1), where commercial usefulness played a central role in development. The main advantage of MED1 is that uncertain knowledge can be processed with a great deal of flexibility.

6.3.1 The Concept of Knowledge Representation and Knowledge Processing

The terms and concepts in this section (diagnosis, rule, question, procedure, etc.) cannot be discussed separately. Therefore, it is unavoidable for some terms to be used before they have been completely described, or for some concepts to be introduced "piecemeal." Hence, the reader is advised to first skim through this section quickly, then go back and read it thoroughly.

The basic unit of knowledge representation in MED1 is the rule. A rule is made up of conditions, which refer to "questions," and actions, which determine the plausibility of diagnoses. A question essentially consists of a question number, the question text, and response alternatives, e.g.,:

F1   Are you looking for an expensive or an inexpensive car?

W1   inexpensive

W2   expensive

Questions requiring a numerical answer are also allowed, such as:

F2   What is the maximum you want to spend?

A condition tests whether a specific response was selected for a question or whether the numerical answer to a question lies within a specific range.

(F1 W1)   tests whether the car should be inexpensive.

(F2 0 18,000)   tests whether the car should cost less than $18,000.

In order to describe the form that actions take in a rule, we must first consider the concept of "diagnosis" and the processing of uncertain knowledge in MED1:

Diagnoses are identified mainly by their name and an identification code consisting of the letter "D" and a number (e.g., "D1 Myocardial Infarction"). In order to test the diagnoses, MED1 utilizes forward- and backward-chaining rules, which differ in the syntax of their actions. Forward-chaining rules, which will be described in more detail later, are used primarily to generate a list of suspected diagnoses at the beginning of the consultation.

The user must first answer a series of general questions, which are evaluated by the forward-chaining rules. As the result of this evaluation, the diagnoses are entered into a list, called an "agenda," arranged according to the degree of speculation. The most likely diagnosis is then tested using backward-chaining rules. The goal of the consultation is to prove, by means of rules, the certainty of one diagnosis from a list of several. If this is not possible, MED1 stops the consultation and outputs a list of diagnoses arranged according to the degree of certainty. The term "certainty" is not to be confused with the concept of confidence factors as used in mathematical probability; rather, it is a measure of the confidence that can be placed in a particular diagnosis.

The certainty of a diagnosis is expressed in terms of a "certainty category." There are seven categories for classifying a diagnosis: impossible, next to impossible, unlikely, neutral, probable, highly probable, certain.

In the actions of a rule, a point system is applied to the diagnoses, whereby the points accumulate and ultimately determine the category of the diagnosis. For each diagnosis, a special list called "Evaluation" can be used to define the totals assigned to each category.

Example

The evaluation list

(-90 -40 -20 20 60 150)

is assigned to the diagnosis "D1 Myocardial Infarction."

This means:

Total points less than -90   category "impossible."

Total points between -90 and -40:   "   "next to impossible"

. . . . .

Total points greater than 150:   "   "certain"

This method allows the expert system developer full control over the evidence-reinforcement mechanism (assessing the plausibility of a diagnosis). Other shells use a number between -1 and 1, calculated according to a fixed set of rules, as a measure of the plausibility of a diagnosis. The evaluation scale used in MED1 can be defined by the user. The flexibility of this method is illustrated in the example below.

Example

Evaluation scale: (-100 -90 -80 80 90 100)

Effect   Suppose each rule adds or subtracts 10 points to/from the "account" of the diagnosis. A large number of rules would have to fire before the diagnosis is regarded as probable. In other words, many indications will have to coincide for the diagnosis to be even considered (e.g., because it very seldom holds true). The interval between "probable" and "certain" is quite small. A different evaluation scale (e.g., (-1000 -100 -10 10 100 1000)) has a correspondingly different effect.

The example also indicates that negative point values may be assigned to rules, e.g., to account for the fact that some symptoms may also work against a diagnosis.

A list of suspected diagnoses, as mentioned above, is generated analogously. Forward-chaining rules assign "speculation points" to diagnoses, which are then entered into "speculation categories." Speculation points and speculation categories are not to be confused with (certainty) points and certainty categories.

A typical forward-chaining rule has the following format:

R1 ((F1 W1)) ((SPEC D7 100))

The keyword SPEC identifies rule R1 as a forward-chaining rule, which assigns speculation points. If the user has answered question F1 by selecting answer W1, rule R1 adds 100 points to the speculation-point count of diagnosis D7.

According to the predefined scale (100 200 300), speculation points are converted to the speculation categories "nil," "possible," "of interest," and "of great interest." A diagnosis with a total of 250 speculation points would fall under the category "of interest."

All forward-chaining rules and questions which should be used in generating the list of suspected diagnoses must be entered in a list called FIRST (e.g., FIRST (F1 R1)). When the processing of the rules and questions in FIRST has been completed (i.e., suspected diagnoses have been generated), the verification of suspected diagnoses begins, i.e., processing of all backward-chaining rules that make reference to the diagnosis in the highest speculation class.

For difficult diagnoses, the number of rules can, of course, be very large. Therefore, it may not be appropriate to apply all the rules if the evaluation of some of them has already established that the diagnosis in question is "impossible" or "unlikely." In such a case, the user would have to deal with unnecessary questions. To counteract this problem, the number of backward-chaining rules that assign points to diagnoses are grouped into several "procedures." After all the rules of a given procedure have been processed, the corresponding diagnosis is assigned to a certainty category, based on its current points. The diagnosis can then be assigned a new place in the agenda (e.g., lose priority). The speculation-points account is cleared at the beginning of the verification step, since the results of a verification - even incomplete results - are more informative than the results of the generation of suspected diagnoses.

As can be seen, the agenda contains untested diagnoses (according to speculation category) as well as partially-tested diagnoses (according to certainty category). The two categories are sorted as follows:

W7 W6 AZ3 W5 AZ2 W4 AZ1

W7 through W4 are the certainty categories "certain" through "neutral": AZ3 through AZ1 are the speculation categories "of great interest" through "possible."

After a procedure is processed, the agenda is resorted and the diagnosis in the highest category is tested further. Procedures do not have names, only an identification code in the form Pxy, where x is the number of the associated diagnosis and y is an arbitrary letter. Thus, the procedures for diagnosis D1 are designated P1a, P1b, etc.

A typical backward-chaining rule reads as follows:

R2   ((F1 W1))   ((ADD P1a 100))

The keyword ADD identifies backward-chaining rules. If answer W1 was selected in response to question F1, then rule R2 adds 100 points to the point count of diagnosis D1, which is associated with procedure P1a.

MED1 utilizes both forward-chaining and backward-chaining rules.

Forward-chaining rules are used for generating lists of suspected diagnoses; backward-chaining rules are used for testing the suspected diagnoses. In the generation of suspected diagnoses (i.e., at the beginning of the consultation), all the questions listed in FIRST are asked, and then evaluated by the forward-chaining rules, likewise listed in FIRST.

To control the testing of suspected diagnoses, MED1 has an agenda containing untested or partially-tested diagnoses. The test is always performed on the highest-ranking diagnosis. The rules associated with a particular diagnosis, i.e., the rules that assign points to this diagnosis (if applicable), may be distributed over several procedures. After all rules of a particular procedure have been evaluated, the agenda must be resorted. The diagnosis just tested may drop in priority, giving other diagnoses an opportunity to be tested.

The consultation ends when a diagnosis has reached the certainty category "certain"; when a diagnosis is "highly probable" and all other diagnoses are not better than "neutral"; or when no more rules can be applied. Furthermore, the user can terminate the consultation on his own at any time, or force the continuation of a consultation, even though a diagnosis has already proved to be "certain" (e.g., if a patient has more than one illness).

Figure 6.8 illustrates the relationships.

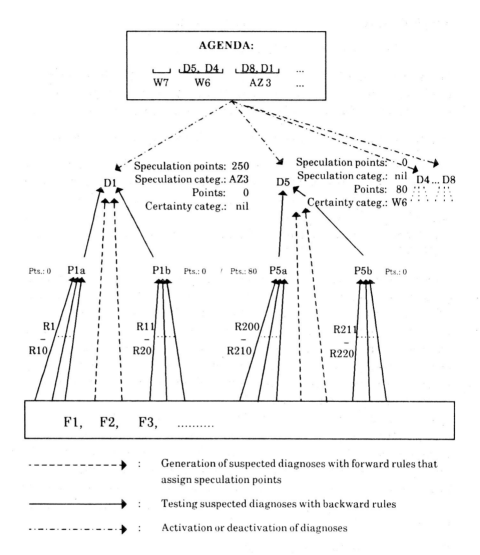

Figure 6.8: Testing of Suspected Diagnoses

As can be seen in the figure, diagnosis D1 has 250 speculation points, but has not yet been tested. D5 has already been partially tested (P5a processed, class AZ cleared) and has been assigned to the certainty category W6 ("highly probable"). Since D5 is at the top of the agenda, this diagnosis is processed further, i.e., the rules of procedure P5b are processed next.

6.3.2 Example of a Knowledge Base

The problem used in this example is already known from the description -of the KEE tool: the expert system is to give advice to a potential car buyer (in Germany), by asking him three questions concerning price, type of engine, and origin of the desired car, and then making a specific suggestion as to which car he should buy.

The three questions can be stated explicitly in MED1:

F1 Are you looking for an expensive or an inexpensive car?
    W1   inexpensive
    W2   expensive

F2 What type of engine do you want?
    W1   diesel
    W2   gasoline

F3 Are you looking for a German or a foreign car?
    W1   foreign
    W2   German

In MED1 terminology, every purchase suggestion becomes a diagnosis:

D1 VW Golf
D2 VW Golf D
D3 R-5
D4 R-5-GLD
D5 BMW 520
D6 BMW 520td
D7 SAAB
D8 SAAB D

The same evaluation scale is used for all diagnoses:
(-90 -40 -20 20 60 150).

A procedure must then be defined for each diagnosis, to which the backward-chaining rules can refer:

P1a, P2a, P3a, P4a, P5a, P6a, P7a, P8a

Only one procedure is needed for each diagnosis, since the number of rules per diagnosis will be small.

Now the rules:

At the beginning of the consultation the expert system must generate the list of suspected diagnoses; i.e., it asks the user a question and then considers only a few diagnoses that are of interest.

The forward-chaining rules R1 and R2 are defined as follows:

R1   ((F1 W1))   ((SPEC D1 250)   (SPEC D2 250)

(SPEC D3 250)   (SPEC D4 250))

R2   ((F1 W2))   ((SPEC D5 250)   (SPEC D6 250)

(SPEC D7 250)   (SPEC D8 250))

The FIRST list must then read as follows:

(F1, R1, R2)

This means that the expert system asks question F1 and, depending on the user's answer, designates either the diagnoses D1, D2, D3, D4 or the diagnoses D5, D6, D7, D8 as "of interest " by assigning 250 speculation points to these diagnoses.

To test the four diagnoses of interest, 16 backward-chaining rules are needed. Four of these are, for example:

R3   ((F2 W1))   ((ADD D2 100))

R4   ((F3 W2))   ((ADD D2 100))

R5   ((F2 W1))   ((ADD D4 100))

R6   ((F3 W1))   ((ADD D4 100))

The other 12 rules are written analogously for the six cars not dealt with in rules R3 through R6.

If the user responded to question F1 with the answer "W1 inexpensive," then the diagnosis "D2 VW Golf D" is among those tested. Before rules R3 and R4 can be applied the user must answer questions F2 and F3. If he responds to F2 with "W1 diesel" and to F3 with "W1 foreign," then diagnosis D2 is assigned only 100 points from Rule 3 and classified as "highly probable." When diagnosis "D4 R-5-GLD" is tested, two rules fire (R5 and R6); diagnosis D4 then receives 200 points and is placed in the "certain" category, thereby ending the consultation.

The listing below documents the execution of a consultation.

```
Are you looking for an expensive or an inexpensive car?
1   inexpensive                    2   expensive
Answer 1
Price: inexpensive

Are you looking for a German or a foreign car?
1   foreign                        2   German
Answer 2
Origin: German

What type of engine do you want?
1   diesel                         2   gasoline
Answer 2
Engine type: gasoline
****************************************************************
These are the results:

Final diagnoses
Highly probable                         D1: VW-GOLF

The following possibilities have not yet been fully
examined:

8th class                               D3: R-5

8th class                               D4: R-5-GLD

You have the following options:

F        Continue the session; process all indications
V        Correct answers
Z        Scroll
S        Display all possible diagnoses
.
.
.
```

6.3.3 Additional Notes On Knowledge Representation

The basic concepts of MED1 presented thus far are enhanced by numerous features which allow the knowledge engineer more freedom when designing a knowledge base. Some of these features are described briefly here:

– Forward-chaining rules can be used not only for generating speculations (keyword "SPEC"), but also for testing the speculations. In this case, the rules must contain the keyword "FADD", and the points are added directly to the count for a diagnosis (without going through a procedure). After each procedure is executed, MED1 checks whether the conditions of a FADD rule have been satisfied.

– "Ask next" is another mechanism (like the procedure concept) for preventing inconsistent and seemingly haphazard questioning by the expert system. Each question (e.g., F1) can be supplemented with a list of other questions (e.g., "Ask next (F2 F3)"), which are to be asked immediately after the first question. In the example, questions F2 and F3 are asked immediately after question F1, even if F2 and F3 do not occur in the rules being processed. This ensures that related information is obtained by asking related questions, even if the expert system ends up with more information than is actually necessary at the moment.

– "Intermediate variables" are equal to questions in importance, and are used essentially for arithmetical linking of answers given to several numerical questions. For example, the intermediate variable "Z1 Mileage in miles/gal" can be calculated from the answers to the questions "F1 How many miles have you driven since you last filled the tank?" and "F2 How many gallons of fuel have you used since then?".

– "Technical investigations" are special procedures that can be supplied with preconditions. Before the rules of a technical investigation are evaluated (the first of these rules generally refers to a question of the form "Please perform test XY; what is the result?"), the preconditions must first be satisfied; the cost of the investigation as compared to the benefit is assessed in this way, and special risks are listed (e.g., it is not advisable to subject a patient who has suffered a myocardial infarction to a stress test).

– In some cases, it makes sense to group content-related diagnoses under one name. MED1 provides the "general diagnosis" for this purpose. The general diagnosis contains the procedures whose rules are to be applied the same way to all specific diagnoses. After all the procedures in the general diagnosis have been processed, the point total is transferred to the specific diagnoses. Each of these can then be examined more closely with their own procedures.

6.3.4 User Interface

Since the BS2000-version of MED1 was developed for a line-oriented screen, its operation is not nearly as convenient as that of the other shells (S.1, KEE, etc.), which provide the user with windows and mouse-activated menus. MED1 also lacks graphics-based trace options, which can be used to continuously follow the application of rules during the course of a consultation.

Nevertheless, MED1 does have an explanation component and several other functions that can be called when the expert system asks a question.

Before the user answers the question, he can

– have the rules and facts (answers to questions) which led to the current question displayed (this serves as an explanation component);

– change the answer to a previous question, if necessary by requesting the output of all questions asked thus far;

– have information about the current status of the expert system displayed (order of priority of the diagnoses in the agenda, etc.);

– terminate the session with STOP (in this case, it is not necessary to answer the question).

6.3.5 Summary

As is known, MED1 is a shell designed specifically for medical diagnosis. Expert knowledge is represented exclusively in the form of rules. Knowledge relating to the objects in the problem area can be entered in the expert system only during a consultation, by answering questions.

This gives rise to several difficulties in designing an expert system for technical diagnosis, e.g., fault diagnosis in defective mainframe computers. Here, it would be advantageous if the expert system included, from the very beginning, knowledge about the relationships between components and modules of the computer system (KEE accomplishes this by means of units and slots). In fields other than medicine, it is not always mandatory to have only one, clear-cut diagnosis. Generally, several suspect modules are exchanged so that the defective part can be deduced from the changes in the fault profile (or from the absence of the fault). For a sick person, the replacement of "parts," of course, is considered only in an emergency (and even then not for test purposes). Procedural knowledge (e.g., LISP code) cannot be integrated into a MED1 knowledge base. Instead, it must be implemented by means of a complex set of rules.

One of the most important advantages of MED1 is that the expert system developer can exercise a great deal of control over the evidence-reinforcement mechanism.

In practice, however, this flexible form of evidence reinforcement has its drawbacks:
In order to define a new rule, the expert system developer must first take into consideration all other rules associated with the same diagnosis, and also the evaluation scale used for the diagnosis.
Otherwise, he runs the risk that the new rule may have inadvertent consequences. (Perhaps the new rule assigns one point too many in a given situation, so that the diagnosis is classified as category "certain" instead of "highly probable" - not exactly an insignificant difference).

Despite all of its limitations, MED1 is an important shell: it runs on conventional mainframes and therefore requires no dedicated hardware (LISP machine or the like).

6.4 LOOPS

LOOPS (LISP-based Object-Oriented Programming System) is a programming tool which is based on the LISP dialect Interlisp-D and which runs on dedicated LISP machines.

LOOPS extends LISP to include object-, rule-, and access-oriented programming capabilities (see "active values" below and the section "Knowledge Representation"). LOOPS supports the definition of the following:

- Classes

  Classes are used for abstract descriptions of identical or similar objects. Classes, in turn, can be grouped into higher-level super-classes. In this way, knowledge can be arranged in a hierarchical structure. The described objects are instances of the classes.

- Class Variables and Instance Variables

  Class descriptions contain both class variables and instance variables. Class variables describe the attributes of a class; they have the same value for all instances of the class. Instance variables describe the individual instances, and can therefore assume a different value for every instance. Class and instance variables can be defined as "active values": if LOOPS accesses these values for reading or writing, a function is called. Active values are frequently also referred to as "demons."

- Methods

  LISP functions, or "methods," are incorporated in class definitions; they describe how an object should respond to a received message.

- Inheritance Mechanisms

  The inheritance mechanisms transfer information from classes to subclasses. This reduces the amount of writing effort required in the representation of similar objects, and supports the consistency of data when changes are made.

- Rules

  The user can define rules; these can be grouped into *rule sets*. The user retains full control over rule processing. LOOPS does not provide an inference mechanism.

- Gauges

  Gauges are indicators that make it possible to visualize the values of variables in different ways (e.g., via digital displays or graphic "direct-reading instruments"). They are defined by a series of classes (which are not part of the actual LOOPS kernel).

- Browser

  LOOPS is generally run via a graphic interface, in this case a browser and menues. A browser entails the representation of information in the form of graphs. LOOPS has a predefined class browser, which represents the hierarchical structure of the classes. The user can also create his own browsers for his applications (Figure 6.9).

- Layers of the Knowledge Base

  Every change made in the knowledge base is treated as a new "layer" built on the existing information. The user can decide which version he wants to use, which facilitates experimental changes.
  In addition to maintaining different versions, LOOPS supports the maintenance of a global knowledge base.

- Individual Work Environments

  The user determines the objects, their relationships, and the sequence in which the knowledge base is to be processed, on a case-by-case basis.

The features offered by Interlisp-D can be implemented with few restrictions.

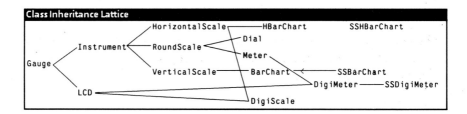

Figure 6.9:   Example of a Class Browser

7 Example: EXPS.MASTERMIND

7.1 The "Mastermind" Game

Several variations of the "Mastermind" game are known. The expert
system EXPS.MASTERMIND implements the following variant:

1. The user specifies a sequence of four colors from the following group:

    r (red), g (green), b (blue), y (yellow), p (pink), o (orange)

    Example

    User: [o,p,r,b].

2. The system attempts to "guess" this sequence of colors.

    Example

    EXPS.MASTERMIND: [r,g,b,y].

3. The user states which colors

    –   are correct and in the correct position in the sequence ("s"),

    –   are correct, but in the wrong position in the sequence ("w"),

    –   are incorrect ("n").

    The last statement is necessary because EXPS.MASTERMIND always expects a list containing four elements.

    Example

    ```
    User:      [w,w,n,n].
    ```

4. Steps 2 and 3 are repeated until either

    –   the system guesses the correct combination, or

    –   the system does not guess the combination by the 8th round.

    Example

    ```
    EXPS.MASTERMIND: [g,r,p,o].
    User:            [w,w,w,n].
    EXPS.MASTERMIND: [r,p,o,b].
    User:            [s,s,w,w].
    EXPS.MASTERMIND: [o,p,r,b].
    User:            [s,s,s,s].
    ```

7.2 Functional Design

EXPS.MASTERMIND was designed with the goal of providing an expert system which is simple, yet interesting to use. The system is particularly useful for demonstrating some of the basic paradigms which are important for the implementation of expert systems.

EXPS.MASTERMIND consists of the following components.

- The **knowledge base**, in the form of a table with several access and modification functions;

- A **blackboard**, used as a dynamic knowledge base;

- An **inference mechanism** based on production rules;

- An **explanation component**;

- A **main task** for controlling the dialog conducted via the user interface.

- *Knowledge Base*

  In principle, the knowledge base of EXPS.MASTERMIND can contain any type of structure. Special support is provided for a table-oriented knowledge base in the form of several incarnation, access, and update functions. These functions provide general support for the creation of board games.

- *Blackboard*

  The blackboard is used by the inference mechanism to store intermediate of final results of inference, or to record speculations which are to be considered later in the consultation.

Entries are made in the blackboard when specific rules "fire." These rules are called:

– **Demons** or

– **Heuristics.**

Blackboard structure:

Last Answer	Conclusions	Vague Results	Assumptions	Contributions

– The "last answer" field provides quick access to the last entry made by the user and the last decision made by the system. In principle, the inference mechanism can access all previous decisions and information through the knowledge base.

– "Conclusions" are definitive results deduced by the inference mechanism, which can be used in subsequent decision-making. "Conclusions" can only be added; they cannot be modified during a consultation.

– "Vague results" are deduced results which restrict the set of possible answers. The cardinality of this set is greater than 1.

– If the inference mechanism supplies only vague results, "assumptions" can be formulated, which must then be verified or proved wrong.

– If an optimal step cannot be deduced from the previous conclusions and assumptions, it is advantageous to record all possible alternatives, evaluate them, and select the "best" alternative. These tasks are handled by the heuristic rules (see Section 7.3).

● *Inference Mechanism*

The inference mechanism is based on the programming language PROLOG which, in turn, is based on production rules (see Section 5.1). The inference mechanism first activates the demons (see Section 7.3). The firing demon then writes

– conclusions,
– vague results
– assumptions

into the blackboard. The subsequently activated heuristics access the blackboard entries and determine the next move in the game.

● *Explanation Component*

The explanation component uses only information from the blackboard.

This component supplies the following information:

– Course of the game

– Blackboard
　　(conclusions
　　vague results
　　assumptions
　　contributions)

– Justification of decisions regarding moves made in the game.

Example

Below is the explanation for the example described in section 7.1:

```
* * * SIEMENS E X P S . M A S T E R M I N D  K D AP 332 * * *
* * *     k. bauer, u. brossmann, m. drexler, l. pluemer  * * *
```

```
* * * * *    explanation for the following game sequence   * *
                                                            *
```

o	p	r	b				
r	p	o	b	s	s	w	w
g	r	p	o	w	w	w	n
r	g	b	y	w	w	n	n

```
blackboard :
conclusion(color,o,d4,1)
conclusion(color,p,d4,1)
conclusion(colors,[r,p,o,b],d3,3)
conclusion(npos,[r,1],d4,1)
conclusion(npos,[g,2],d4,1)
conclusion(npos,[b,3],d4,1)
conclusion(npos,[y,4],d4,1)
conclusion(npos,[g,1],d9,2)
conclusion(npos,[r,2],d9,2)
conclusion(npos,[p,3],d9,2)
conclusion(npos,[o,4],d9,2)
vague(colors,[b,y],d9,2)
assumption(move,[r,g,b,y],d1,0,false)
assumption(move,[r,p,o,b],d9,2,_4245)
assumption(move,[g,r,o,p],d4,1,false)
assumption(move,[r,p,b,o],d3,3,_4245)
contribution([g,r,p,o],[[],[h2,[conclusion(color,[g,at_place,1],
h1,n),
conclusion(color,[r,at_place,2],h1,n),
conclusion(color,[p,at_place,3],d4,1),
conclusion(color,[o,at_place,4],d4,1)]]],1)
contribution([r,p,o,b],[],2)
contribution([o,p,r,b],[[],[h2,[conclusion(color,[o,at_place,1],
d4,1),
conclusion(color,[p,at_place,2],d4,1),
conclusion(color,[r,at_place,3],d3,3),
conclusion(color,[b,at_place,4],d3,3)]]],3)
```

The following demons drew conclusions from the 3rd move : [d3]
d3 leaves two places the same and changes the others
demon d3 deduced : colors [r,p,o,b]
demon d3 assumed : move [r,p,b,o]
after move number 3, the following points were considered:
 heuristic h2 : combination change performed.
    d4 deduced before the 1st move : color [o,at_place,1]
    d4 deduced before the 1st move : color [p,at_place,2]
    d3 deduced before the 3rd move : color [r,at_place,3]
    d3 deduced before the 3rd move : color [b,at_place,4]

The following demons drew conclusions from the 2nd move : [d9]
d9 adds a new color and changes the other 3
demon d9 deduced : npos [g,1]
demon d9 deduced : npos [r,2]
demon d9 deduced : npos [p,3]
demon d9 deduced : npos [o,4]
demon d9 speculated : colors [b,y]
demon d9 assumed : move [r,p,o,b]
after move number 2, the following points were considered:

The following demons drew conclusions from the 1st move : [d4]
d4 changes 2 colors and adds 2 new ones
demon d4 deduced : color o
demon d4 deduced : color p
demon d4 deduced : npos [r,1]
demon d4 deduced : npos [g,2]
demon d4 deduced : npos [b,3]
demon d4 deduced : npos [y,4]
demon d4 assumed : move [g,r,o,p]
after move number 1, the following points were considered:
 heuristic h2 : combination change performed.
    h1 deduced before the nth move : color [g,at_place,1]
    h1 deduced before the nth move : color [r,at_place,2]
    d4 deduced before the 1st move : color [p,at_place,3]
    d4 deduced before the 1st move : color [o,at_place,4]

Expert Systems

- *Main task*

  The main task

  - controls the dialog with the system via the user interface during consultation, and

  - terminates the session after a successful consultation or as a result of other termination criteria.

  The main task is implemented in the form of a loop, which includes the following:

  - Supplying user information and requesting user input;

  - Checking user input for specific syntactic (e.g. presence of the period at the end of an input) and semantic criteria (e.g., information function regarding to the status of the game);

  - Partial updating of the static and dynamic knowledge base;

  - System decisions (conflict resolution) regarding the next step, and renewed updating of the knowledge bases (calling the inference mechanism);

  - Terminating or reentering the loop.

7.3 Construction of Rules

In the rules of EXPS.MASTERMIND. a distinction is made between

– demons and

– heuristic rules (Figure 7.1)

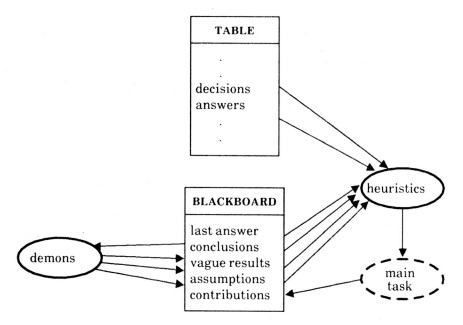

Figure 7.1: Read and Write Access by Demons and Heuristics

- Demons

  Demons are particularly simple, forward-directed rules; they "fire" precisely at the time that their preconditions are met.

  Structure

  di : <Condition> → <Action>

  where
  di   = Demon designation
  Condition   = Conditions under which di is to fire,
  Action   = Entries in the blackboard.

  Example

  ```
  d3 :- precond(s,s,w,w), !, last_decision(L),
  conclude(d3,colors,L),

      equal2_change2(L,NEWDECISION), assumpt(d3,move,NEWDECISION),-.
  ```

  Demon d3 fires when the last decision (the most recent move in the game) was evaluated as [s,s,w,w]. The actions are:

  – Entry of the conclusion

    ```
    conclusion(colors,< last move>,d3,<move number>)
    ```

    into the blackboard.

  – Assumption that only the positions of two colors need to be exchanged.

  – Entry of the assumption into the blackboard.

  Demons are used in EXPS.MASTERMIND to enter possible

  – *conclusions,*
  – *vague results* or
  – *assumptions*

  into the blackboard for each user response. This process makes it easier to formulate heuristic rules (see p. 182), which then build on these results.

Format of Conclusions

$$
\text{conclusion(}
\begin{Bmatrix}
\text{color,} <\text{Color}> \\
\text{colors,} <\text{Move}> \\
\text{npos,[} <\text{Color}>, <\text{Position}>]
\end{Bmatrix}
, <\text{Demon}>, \\
<\text{Number}>)
$$

where

Color	=	color
Move	=	proposed move in the game
Position	=	position in the move
Demon	=	demon designation
Number	=	number of the move for which the demon was activated.

Notes Regarding the Formats

–   Braces ({ }) indicate alternative entries.

–   A pair of braces followed by periods means that the expression inside the braces can be repeated any number of times (separated by commas).

–   An expression in angle brackets (< >) is application-dependent.

–   All symbols occuring in the formats (with the exception of braces ar angle brackets) are part of the format itself (e.g., parentheses or square brackets, commas, single periods, expressions not enclosed in angle brackets).

Format of Vague Results

vague(colors,[<Color> , <Color>], <Demon> , <Number>)

Format of Assumptions

$$\text{assumption(move,} <\text{Move}> , <\text{Demon}> , <\text{Number}> , \begin{cases} \text{color,} <\text{Color}> \\ \text{colors,} <\text{Move}> \\ <\text{uninstantiated variable}> \end{cases}$$

It may be important for demons to fire in a particular sequence. This is especially true if one demon builds on the action of another.

The case may occur where a demon can force a conclusion (e.g., if the user response is [w,w,n,n]). A special type of demon is available for this purpose, which immediately terminates the subsequent procedure after the action, and supplies a result at that time.

Demons which are intended to bring about immediate termination must be identified accordingly.

● Heuristic Rules

Starting with a move proposed by the demons, the heuristic rules attempt to improve on this proposal by utilizing the blackboard information.

The heuristic rules, which are programmed as backward-chaining rules, are grouped under the predicate "decision."

Structure

```
decision(<Move>,<Reason>) : <Condition>
```

where

Move   = decision as to which move should be made

Reason   = reason why the decision <Move> was made

Condition   = conditions which make reference to the entries
                 in the blackboard.

Derivation of the Decisions

1. Suppose that HYP is proposed by a demon as the next move in a game; it is taken from the assumptions in the blackboard. HYP is used as the initial combination for the procedure.

2. The heuristic rule (only one heuristic rule is implemented in EXPS.MASTERMIND) derives a move HEU from HYP.

3. If HEU is identical to HYP, the heuristic rule is activated again.

4. If HEU is identical to an earlier move, HEU is labelled as false. This identification is included in the <Reason> field. The heuristic rule is activated again.

The heuristic rules access conclusions, vague results, and assumptions which are in the blackboard, as well as decisions and user responses to previous moves. Any changes made in the demons' assumptions are written into the blackboard by the main task (contributions).

Format of Contributions

```
contribution(<Move>,<Trace>,<Number>)
```

where

Move	=	move in the game
Trace	=	[{[<heuristic rule >,[{ <structure >}...]]}...] (specification of those heuristic rules which are applied as a result of the specified demon decisions)
Structure	=	special conclusions, vague results or assumptions
Number	=	number of the move for which the heuristic rule was activated

8 Project Experience with SIUX

8.1 Project Overview

The purpose of SIUX (**SIEMENS UDS EX**pert) is to analyze the runtime performance of database applications. The problem of "performance analysis" can be outlined as follows:

Operationally, database applications are very complex. An inefficient implementation of a database application has negative effects on the runtime performance, the reasons for which are not readily apparent to the DB user.

SIUX is an expert system that supports the expert in the optimization of the runtime performance of the Siemens Database System UDS (Universal Database System). SIUX analyzes measured values supplied by a database monitor as well as user responses relating to the problem under consideration. Based on the analysis, recommendations are made on how to eliminate the bottleneck.

SIUX

– calculates expected values for DB performance based on the
  computer configuration and DB application (Figure 8.1);

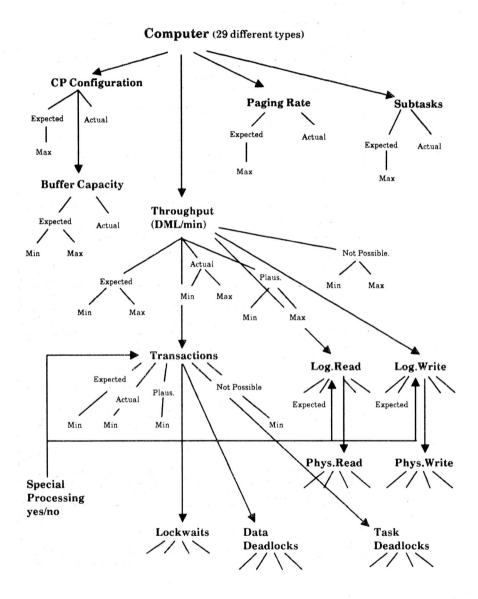

Figure 8.1:   Calculation of Expected Values

SIUX

– supplies diagnoses and makes recommendations for fault correction (Figure 8.2).

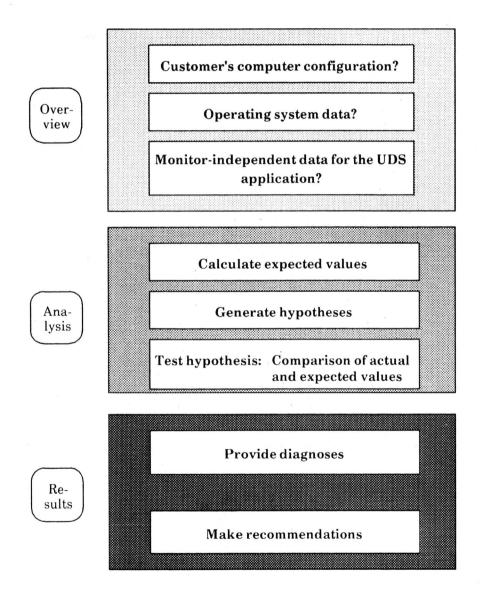

Figure 8.2: Determination of Results

SIUX is highly dialog-oriented. On request, it gives reasons for the questions asked and shows all rules which led to the confirmation or rejection of the diagnoses. If requested, it also provides information as to why it did not make a diagnosis that the user may have suspected (Figure 8.3).

Reasons for a Question

```
NUMBER OF TRANSACTIONS PER SESSION ( = 15 MIN.)? ← System question
```

```
ANSWER =
?   ← User input
THE QUESTION SERVES TO TEST THE DIAGNOSIS PROGRAM_DESIGN_FAULT
PROCEDURE:              PROCEDURE_DIAG71
ACTIVE RULE:
        R710           SPECIAL_PROCESSING_ROUTINES = NO
                       LOG.-READ/PHYS.-READ < 4
                       DML/TRANSACTION < 25
                       DML/TRANSACTION > 10
INTERMEDIATE VARIABLE: DML/TRANSACTION
ACTIVE RULE:
   -  CALCULATION OF DML / TRANSACTIONS
        R7             DML TRANSACTIONS        KNOWN
                       TRANSACTIONS >= 1
QUESTIONS:             TRANSACTIONS
```

Reasons for a Diagnosis

```
D31   ←    User input
REASON FOR D31  -  BUFFER_PARAMETERS_INSUFFICIENT
THE FOLLOWING INDICATIONS SUPPORT THE DIAGNOSIS:
        R310           LOG._READ/PHYS._READ < 4
                       SPECIAL_PROCESSING_ROUTINES - NO
                       PAGING_RATE < PAGING_RATE_UPPER_LIMIT
                       PP-BUFFER <BUFFER_UPPER_LIMIT
THE FOLLOWING RULES WERE NOT (YET) APPLICABLE:
        R311           LOG._READ/PHYS._READ < 15
                       SPECIAL_PROCESSING_ROUTINES -
                       PARTS_LIST_PROCESSING

                       PHONETICIZATION_PROGRAMS, KDBS-APPLICATION

                       PAGING_RATE < PAGING-RATE_UPPER_LIMIT
                       PP-BUFFER < BUFFER_UPPER_LIMIT
        R312           LOG._WRITE/PHYS._WRITE < 1.500000
                       SPECIAL_PROCESSING_ROUTINES - NO
                       PAGING_RATE < PAGING_RATE_UPPER_LIMIT
                       PP_BUFFER < BUFFER_UPPER_LIMIT
```

Figure 8.3:   Example of the Explanation Component

Primary Objectives

The main objective in the development of SIUX was to answer the question:
What significance does expert systems technology have for *commercial applications* in the conventional DP environment?

The SIUX system currently runs under the BS2000 operating system on the general-purpose 7.xxx series computers and on the PC2000. It is presently implemented in INTERLISP based on a modified version of the MED1 shell (F. Puppe, Kaiserslautern University; see Figure 8.4). SIUX analyzes DB applications for approximately 30 different types of computers and their many configuration variants. It can apply 17 different diagnoses, which are generated on the basis of approximately 190 rules (Figure 8.4).

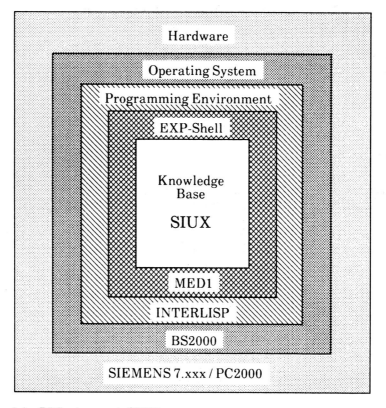

Figure 8.4:   DP Environment of SIUX

8.2 Objectives and Decisions

8.2.1 Initial Situation

The *initial situation* in the area of database applications was characterized by

- a great demand for consulting services to support UDS applications;
- too much variation in the acceptance of the consultants' recommendations on the part of UDS users;
- dependence of the recommendation on the individual consultant

The initial situation for the development of SIUX was characterized as follows:

- The problem existed and the necessary expertise was available.

- Conventional techniques could not be used because the solution of the problem was

    - too imprecise at the beginning of the project;
    - too dynamic (not primarily textbook knowledge, but rather "acquired empirical knowledge").

- The problem was sufficiently complex (combinatorial explosions!).

- Standard situations existed (the individual UDS applications are not "unique," but rather follow generally valid principles).

- Rules and specifiable procedures existed for the specific area.

- There were specialists in the subject area who were ready to make their knowledge available.

- There were users willing to perform early testing of an incomplete system.

- The target group - users and experts alike - had DP experience.

8.2.2 Objectives

In accordance with the initial situation described above, the *objectives* of SIUX development were to:

- reduce the work load of the central UDS support team in Software Customer Service;
- transfer know-how to the regional support teams;
- systematize and save know-how;
- standardize recommendations made to UDS customers;
- increase the transparency of UDS runtime performance for UDS customers;
- make effective use of existing tools for UDS analysis;
- examine the applicability in other areas of system analysis (multiplier effect).

Secondary objectives included the identification and standardization of expert knowledge.

8.2.3 Design Decisions

The situation desribed in the previous sections led to a series of design decisions, the most important of which were:

– Execution under the BS2000 operating system is mandatory

   because

   – the UDS monitor itself, as well as all other UDS tools, run under BS2000;

   – during the initial pilot phase, experts and users should be spared the emotional and financial "burden" of dealing with the unfamiliar AI environment.

– Central pool of knowledge relating to set-up, expansion, and maintenance:
   external users have access via a network.

– The expert system should support, rather than replace, the available experts and tools. The main purpose was a filtering function: the "interesting" cases should continue to be left to the experts.

– The expert system should offer diagnoses, but not practice therapy. Suggestions for subsequent actions are made only in obvious situations.

– In the interest of saving time, little importance was initially attached to an optimal user interface.

8.3   SIUX Development Phases

The following observations are based on the concepts and relationships of expert system techniques as represented and described in Figure 8.5. It must be pointed out that this scheme, which has been modified several times, does not represent a "process technology" in the sense of standard software development.
In addition, checkpoints and objectives were defined for very limited time intervals; these made it possible to monitor progress in the project and to coordinate further proceedings *with all participants.*

In the following discussion, it is assumed that the reader is familiar with the steps outlined in Figure 8.5; the selection is a sampling of the problems encountered by the Knowledge Engineering Team (KE Team) at various stages.

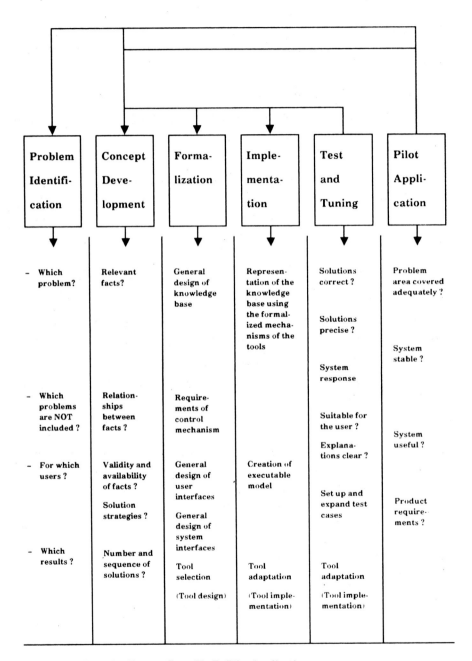

Figure 8.5:   Iterative Process Steps Up To Pilot Application

8.3.1 Shell Selection

Considering the basic design, the destination processors, and the expert system shells available, MED1 was chosen as the shell. The following facts were decisive:

- Basically, MED1 is well-suited for diagnostic purposes;

- The KE team was familiar with the shell - though certain limitations did not become apparent until the project was under way.

- The MED1 developers themselves were available to make modifications in the shell. Because of the physical distance involved, however, this cooperation often was not sufficiently prompt, so that the KE Team itself had to make the necessary changes during the course of the project.

- Initially, little emphasis was placed on a graphics-oriented user interface.

During the course of the project, some basic limitations of the shell became apparent, which ruled out its use for a SIUX *product*. These limitations are:

1. MED1 itself is no more a product than the underlying language, INTERLISP, in which it is implemented. This has predictable effects on runtime reliability and documentation. The MED1 documentation suffered due to the many changes that were implemented; it should have been created completely from scratch and then adapted for each case. This was not possible with the available manpower.
   The inadequate SW documentation had no serious effects on the creation of a prototype, since it was possible to keep track of the project in terms of scope and the number of people directly affected by the shell modifications. This type of situation, however, is not advisable for product development.

2. MED1 is an exclusively diagnosis-oriented shell: While it is possible to link questions of a specific type that are to be asked of the user, according to the principle of progressive detailing, the type of question most frequently used here was not suited for this option in SIUX. Apart from this type of question-chaining, the only structuring principle is the organization of the individual rules around the diagnoses known to the system. In other words, it is practically impossible to implement actions which are not directly linked to a diagnosis. This is also one of the reasons why it is very difficult to run plausibility checks on user input: there is no diagnosis which could be linked, for example, to a warning to the user when a single "suspect" value is entered - the validity of which cannot be determined until run time. A higher-level control mechanism has since been implemented which makes this possible. However, the effort involved is unacceptably disproportionate with the results achieved.

3. With respect to the SIUX problem (primarily interpretation of measured values), MED1's inadequacies in arithmetic functions and in operations which compare numerical values proved to be another weakness. This deficiency has since been eliminated for the most part. However, the user interface in the acquisition component for these functions is still not simple enough to allow the experts themselves to make changes in rules, without a lengthy training period.

4. MED1 is essentially a shell for the knowledge engineer (KE), who can use it to succesfully control the system's behavior - at least as long as no errors occur in the shell. If errors do occur in the shell - and, of course, if modifications are required - a thorough knowledge of INTERLISP is necessary in order to make any improvements. A particular handicap was the fact that MED1 does not have an INTERLISP interface integrated into its design. The possibility of switching directly from MED1 to INTERLISP was indeed made available while the project was in progress, but this facility is intended primarily for troubleshooting, and not for integrating additional functions into MED1. The MED1 concept does not provide for the processing of values generated by functions outside of MED1.

Expert Systems

While the KEs who were expanding the shell did not have a defined interface for functions outside of MED1, the experts and users did not have access to explanations and knowledge base dumps that they could understand without first familiarizing themselves with MED1. For these users, a special interface was provided which was free from internal system details. While this non-KE interface represents only a compromise, experts and users alike have been using it successfully in the meantime. Inexperienced users, however, will find that the SIUX explanations still require some clarification. This is due not so much to the form of representation as to the fact that SIUX knowledge is not based on a causal model of DB behavior, but rather bases the reasoning process on simple connections between observations (see section 8.3.2).

5. Current expert system shells implicitly assume that one-man systems are being developed. Consequently, there is currently no form of SW configuration management (if one disregards the fact that many LISP-based tools, by default, general a new version number for the current file after every write or save operation performed on a knowledge base or shell – resulting in confusion and an immense number of files rather than offering support). This problem is aggravated by the fact that the knowledge base and shell are generally modified by different people at different times; furthermore, because of the dynamics of the knowledge base, it is inevitable that different versions will be undergoing testing at the same time. Since there are currently no effective software management tools available, at least for version administration, the only recourse so far has been strict discipline. The only means of support available to us during the project was the strict separation of the development version and the user version at the "hardware" level: the two versions are implemeted on different computer systems, and the transition from the development system to the user system is made under close supervision following a series of tests.

8.3.2 Development of the Knowledge Base

When the knowledge engineering team began its work, the *problem identification* phase was already completed (by the customer).
Initially, the expert system was to support the analysis of the UDS system in operation (and not, for example, to monitor a special program), with the help of the data supplied by the DB monitor.

Therefore, for all intents and purposes, knowledge acquisition for the KE team began with the *concept development* phase. During this early phase, the problems were mainly on two levels:

– The KE team was not sufficiently familiar with the special problems and terminology of the UDS language (general knowledge about databases was far from sufficient!).

– Individual specialists did not agree on internal work concepts and methods (see Section 8.2.2, secondary objectives). It must be reiterated that generally established textbook knowledge represents only a very small part of SIUX; like most empirical procedures, SIUX represents the opinions of experts which, naturally, are subject to change.

Two simple **examples** may help to clarify the latter point:

● The question of how long and at what time of day the DB monitor should run, in order to supply some of the values to be analyzed by SIUX, was at first tacitly regarded as having been settled. The problem did not become apparent until the first pilot user applied completely different measuring times, which resulted in measured values which SIUX could not process.

- The conversion of statements such as "approximately 20" or "much smaller than" to a numerical range that SIUX could process represented a considerable effort on the part of the UDS experts. This effort would certainly have been reduced if only a single expert had been involved with SIUX. However, this appeared to be neither possible nor practical. On the one hand, the required level of detail and the acceptability of the knowledge could only be achieved through discussions among the subject specialists. On the other hand, it was imperative that the special knowledge was continuously and readily available throughout the course of the project. Since it is well known that the "good" expert is the one that has no time, it is impossible to place the load of creating the contents of the knowledge base on a single expert. Thus, the often heated debate as to whether it is "better" to work with one expert or several seems to be rather an academic issue.

The *formalization* phase suffered greatly from the fact that there is currently no powerful "knowledge editor" available to facilitate the representation of the knowledge, independent of the subsequent implementation tool. Therefore, as soon as a rough design of the overall concept was completed and several rules were defined, the implementation with MED1 was started. Consequently, the "formalization" and "implementation" phases coincided. The advantage of early implementation was that the MED1 "knowledge editor" could be used to structure the output from the knowledge base (e.g., "Show me all the rules for diagnosis A"; or, "Give me all the rules which access fact X"). This also made it possible to recognize and assess the interaction of the individual knowledge components in a dynamic environment at a very early stage.

The disadvantages of this procedure were the following:

– The entire knowledge acquisition process was carried out using MED1 (see Section 6.2), which is not optimal for SIUX.

– The very helpful, structured output from the knowledge base could not be read by the subject specialists without spending additional time (which they did not have, of course) to familiarize themselves with MED1.
Therefore, a parallel documentation package, independent of MED1 representation and written in quasi-natural language, was prepared for the knowledge base in the early stages. While this documentation was easy to read for the experts, it not only involved considerably more effort on the part of the KE team, given the knowledge base dynamics and the complete independence from the MED1 representation, but, more importantly, it was a source of error which is very difficult to control. The path taken by the knowledge, from the expert through the KE team and to the BS2000 operating system, was thus extended by yet another factor, i.e., "external documentation." Consequently, MED1 was modified at a relatively early stage so that knowledge base documentation could be generated from within MED1 itself, in a form that the experts could understand. The importance of this in view of the rapid growth of the knowledge base and the development of a single, relatively simple rule is illustrated in Tables 8.1 and 8.2.

SIUX

SIUX-Version	Computer Types	"Relevant" Questions	Diagnoses	Rules for		
				Dia-gnosis	Expected Values	Plaus. values
1	5	16	7	14 24	+ 10	+ 0
2	5	16	11	16 27	+ 11	+ 0
3	29	19	14	40 75	+ 35	+ 0
4	29	25	15	44 95	+ 51	+ 0
5	29	25	17	44 191	+ 51	+ 96

Table 8.1: Dynamic Structure of Knowledge Base

SIUX

SIUX-Version	Diagnosis/ Diagnoses	Rule(s)
1	Long-running	**If No.Log.Read per DML > Expected value then long-running**
2	Long-running	If No.Log.Read per DML > Expected value **or No.DML per transaction > Expected value** then long-running
3	Long-running	**If (no special processing routines and No.Log.Read per DML > Expected value-1) or (special processing routines and No.Log.Read per DML > Expected value-2)** then long-running **If (no special processing routines and No.DML per transaction > Expected value-1) or (special processing routines and No.DML per transaction > Expected value-2)** then long-running
4	**Long-running DMLA** **Long-running Transactions**	If (no special processing routines and No.Log.Read per DML > Expected value-1) or (special processing routines and No.Log.Read per DML > Expected value-2) **then long-running DML** If (no special processing routines and No.DML per transaction > Expected values-1) or (special processing routines and No.DML per transaction > Expected value-2) **then long-running transactions**

Table 8.2:   Dynamic Structure of Knowledge Base (Rules)

The *test and tuning* phase was integrated into the *pilot applications* phase with only minor delays. The pilot user became involved as soon as the first, albeit weak model executed without software errors. As result, four main problem areas emerged:

1. A test environment was required which permitted both of the following:

   - keeping the knowledge base constant and modifying the cases to be diagnosed, and

   - keeping the cases to be diagnosed constant and modifying the knowledge base.

   In the process, all possible support was to be made available for the test operation, since the KE team had to test for error-free software execution and correct conversion of the knowledge supplied by the experts in MED1, but the accuracy of the *contents* could only be verified by the experts.

   This also meant that a separate user interface to the knowledge base had to be provided for the experts, because the single explanation component originally supplied by MED1 primarily served the knowledge engineer, but was too complicated and incomprehensible for the experts.

2. The pilot users, who were *not* the same individuals as the experts whose know-how constituted the knowledge base, discovered some contexts which had previously not been considered. These were implicitly assumed for the correctness of the rules, but were by no means universally valid. Furthermore, consideration of all the users' computer configurations led to explosive growth of the knowledge base (see Table 8.1).

3. As the knowledge implemented in SIUX became more powerful, new discoveries were made about the relationships between the individual concepts. Some of the requirements which resulted from these findings would not only have meant that the knowledge base would have to be completely restructured – – they were also impossible to implement neatly using the selected shell.

Example 1

It became clear that relationships existed between individual diagnoses which depended on the state of the respective diagnoses at the time of execution (in consultation mode). A method to deal with this situation – not anticipated in SIUX – was implemented in a roundabout way, and admittedly functioned without problem; but because of the small number of such cases in the current system, and its complexity, this does not represent a practical final solution.

Example 2

The users required plausibility checks of input values which went far beyond the syntax checks already implemented. Because of the interdependence of the expected values (see Figure 8.1), the plausibility of an individual value cannot be determined until the time of execution. Another requirement soon arose for a minimum amount of "common sense" on the part of MED1 with regard to the evaluation of the entered values.
Conceptually, these two requirements placed considerable demands on the knowledge base: in effect, the "standard" rule structure had to be overlaid with a second structure, which interpreted amd controlled the input for the "standard" rules (for the resulting requirements on the MED1 shell, see Section 8.3.1).

4. To provide an explanation component which would be truly informative even for inexperienced users, SIUX would have to have a knowledge base built on a causal model of the analysis area. This, however, is not the case: explanations of a diagnosis or system response always consist of AND/OR operations performed on observed phenomena, most of which are very complex, to be sure. The actual "semantics" of these operations, however, is left to the interpretation of the user.

8.4   Experience Gained from the Project

SIUX has achieved its goal of being a useful tool, i.e., one that is actually used, in a domain that had previously been closed to support. This was primarily due to the method used in its development, using a team of committed partners having equal status, consisting of customers, experts, users, and knowledge engineers. All important decisions were made in regularly scheduled meetings of a committee representing all those involved. Below is a description of the various roles played by the participants, which is intended to stress the necessitiy of this rather unconventional approach. Such a method, whether as described here or modified, should be applicable to the development of expert systems in general.

The Customer

In the case of SIUX, the customer had already completed an important phase by providing the problem analysis. He was familiar with the problem area, and was thus prepared to help bridge the "communication gap" between the experts and the knowledge engineers. Throughout the entire course of the project, the customer took responsibility of the coordination of all participants and, particularly, for management support which is indispensable for high-risk projects such as expert systems.

The Expert

The role of the expert, who makes his specialized knowledge available, is determined mainly by two factors. The first depends on the type of knowledge in an expert system; the second, on the technology used in implementing such a system:

–   The expert is responsible for the knowledge in the system, because this knowledge is essentially empirical; he alone must decide on the application and distribution of this knowledge.
    There is some kind of symbiotic relationship between the expert and an expert system. On the one hand, the knowledge in the expert system would quickly become obsolete if the expert did not incorporate any new knowledge. On the other hand, the expert system could be used to show how the experts learned more from the practical application of their knowledge.

– Since a significant part of the knowledge base consists of data which is represented by code in conventional programs, the responsibility for the "code," in this context, is transferred from the "programmer" to the expert. Before he can accept this responsibility, the expert needs a tool which is tailored to his knowledge and which he can use in maintaining a current and accurate knowledge base.

The problem is of considerable importance if the expert system is to be used in commercial applications. Generally, new requirements are placed on the system with each new application; rules are defined, new contexts are formulated, etc. The knowledge engineering team cannot, however, support a system throughout its service life. In the long run there is only one solution to this problem: like the database administrator, there must also be a expert system administrator. This administrator is an *expert* whose task is to maintain the knowledge stored in the system.

The User

As soon as a first working model was available, the pilot users of SIUX were definitely involved in the project. In this way, it was possible to test both MED1 and the knowledge base at an early stage in an application environment. From the very beginning, an operational infrastructure was available for system testing, which made it possible to let SIUX mature while in operation. The users were also able to relate their experience gained in a wide diversity of SIUX applications which were not originally planned; in addition to its originally planned function, "Analysis of DB Runtime Problems," SIUX is now being used

- for on-the-job training for beginners;
- by experienced DB users for simulation purposes;
- by first-time DB users to strengthen their line of reasoning in discussions with the experts setting up the DB;
- by the DB experts themselves;
    - as a "dynamic reference," which retains knowledge about older DB versions still in use, while the experts are focusing their attention on a new DB generation;

- for checking the experts' knowledge, in terms of practical relevance. They utilize the system's facility to show, if requested, the rules that did not fire for a given diagnosis. This provides information about the sensitivity and robustness of the DB system under investigation.

These diverse applications made considerable demands on the system, not all of which could be met:

Example 1

To the surprise of the developers, SIUX was used from the very beginning to confirm that the UDS application contained *no* detectable errors. Since SIUX analysis, however, tended towards the diagnosis of faulty operation in a DB application, the user received, in normal cases, nothing more than a short message that nothing could be found. This unsatisfactory situation was resolved so that when the user entered measured values from his DB application which were within the expected range, he received immediate positive feedback during the course of the consultation.

Example 2

Since SIUX offers the option of selectively changing individual user entries at the end of a consultation and then recalculating all the diagnoses (a very important option for convenient testing), this function was used from the very start for simulation purposes ("What if I could increase the DML throughput by 50% ?"). However, SIUX was not implemented with this objective, so it remains solely the user's responsibility to ensure the logical consistency of his entries when using fictitious values. A universal solution to this problem would be beyond the scope of SIUX, at both the shell and the knowledge base levels. The only support possible, apart form a specific warning about this problem in the operating manual, was the introduction of plausibility checks at conspicuous points.

The Knowledge Engineer

The primary responsibilities of the knowledge engineer are the structuring and representation of the problem domain in a model which, by means of a shell, can be transferred to a computer, executed, and tested. Even if better shells were available for supporting the acquisition of knowledge, the expert would not be in a position to build the knowledge base without additional assistance:

- In doing so, he would restrict his very scarce time even further.

- In general, he is not as well equipped as the knowledge engineer to abstract his procedures to such an extent that they can be formalized.

- The selection and adaptation of a suitable tool requires development experience which the expert usually does not have.

- The knowledge engineer is frequently needed as a catalyst to maintain the dialog between the experts.

This assumes, on the one hand, that the knowledge engineer is flexible enough to respond at all times to the demands of experts and users; on the other hand, he must also be able to point out the consequences of individual users' wishes on the entire system.

Therefore, the knowledge engineer must

- offer *more* than mere programming quality; he must make it possible for the expert and user to work closely together with him on the development of the system;

- realize that he is not developing an applications program, but rather a quasi-intelligent tool for experts. It is his resonsibility to select or create the appropriate shell for the experts so that they can test and maintain the knowledge base;

– be able to distinguish between the needs of the experts and those of the users. It is his responsibility to create the individual user interfaces for both types of users.

Summary

– Decisive factors in the success of SIUX were the early involvement of pilot users and the role of the experts as the "owners" of the knowledge base instead of simply being the suppliers of the knowledge. Most of the requirements for the installed tool first become known during the creation and operation of the knowledge base. The most important requirement of a tool, therefore, is ease of adaptation to changing demands.

– The currently available explanation and knowledge-acquisition components do not allow the experts to build and modify the knowledge base without having to invest considerable time in familiarizing themselves with the tool. Since only experts can maintain the knowledge base in the long run, they must be provided with special tools.
Software support is urgently needed for the management of system variants (tool *and* knowledge base) currently under development as well as those in use, so that the software for these expert systems remains manageable, even in the field.

– The users of the expert system SIUX are thus far very satisfied with the expertise supplied. All involved are therefore justified in concluding that SIUX is a viable expert system.

A   Appendices

A.1   Overview of Individual Tools

The tables on the following pages list some tools in alphabetical order.

Abbreviations

CMU   Carnegie-Mellon University
MIT   Massachusetts Institute of Technology
PARC   Palo Alto Research Center
SRI   Stanford Research Institute
SU   Stanford University

Name of Tool	Knowledge Representation	Special Application	Company/ Institution	Remarks
ACTORS	Objects are "actors" and can communicate with other "actors"	Research in data manipulation via "message passing"	MIT	AI programming language
AGE	Frameworks, e.g., backward chaining, blackboard	Development of frameworks for control mechanisms	SU	Program development environment
AIMDS				Knowledge representation language
AL/X		Errors diagnosis; used in the evaluation of expert systems	University of Edinburgh	Shell
ANALYSE N PLUS		Project analysis, cost and time estimates (planning)	Business Information Techniques	Program development system
APES	Prolog terms		Imperial College, London	Shell for PROLOG expert systems

Name of Tool	Knowledge Representation	Special Application	Company/ Institution	Remarks
ARBY		Hardware fault diagnosis	Smart Sytems Technology	Design language shell, written in FranzLISP
ART	Production system	Inference/Automated Reasoning Tool		Shell
BLOBS	Blackboards	Air defense	Cambridge Consultants Ltd.	Program development system
BRAND-X			MIT	AI programming language
CENTAUR	Production rules, prototypes (frame-like data structure)	Monitoring of pulmonary functions	SU	Shell
CRYSTAL	Production sytem		Intelligent Environments, Ltd.	Shell
CSRL	Concept hierarchies	Medical diagnosis	Ohio State University	Knowledge representation language
CONNIVER	Production rules		MIT	AI programming language implemented in MACLISP
EMYCIN	Cf. Chapter 6	Cf. Section 2.1.1, MYCIN	SU	Shell
Epitool			Epitec	Shell
ESE			IBM	Shell
EXPERT	Taxanomic and causal knowledge networks	Ophtalmology, geology	Rutgers University/ University of Missouri	Shell implemented in FORTRAN
EXPERT-EASE		Diagnostic problems	ESI-Intell. Terminals	Shell
FRL	Frames	Error diagnosis	Univ. of Edinburgh	Interpretative knoledge representation language, written in LISP
FUZZY				AI programming language

Name of Tool	Knowledge Representation	Special Application	Company/Institution	Remarks
HEARSAY III	Pattern-action rules, frames, inheritance hierarchies, blackboards	Cf. Appendix A.2: HEARSAY II	University of Southern California	Shell development based on speech recognition research NOTE: Interlisp predecessor of ART
HRPL	Frames, inheritance mechanisms	Detection of technical errors in the production of integrated circuits	Hewlett Packard	Shell
IN-ATE		Fault diagnosis for techn. devices	Automated Reasoning Corp.	Shell in LISP and PASCAL
INSIGHT 2	Rule system		Level Five Research	Program development environment: VAX and PCs with MS DOS
KAS Knowledge Acquisition System	Inference rules and semantic networks	Cf. Appendix A.2: PROSPECTOR	SRI	Editing system written in Interlisp; predecessor of AL/X
KDS	Rule system	For PCs	KDS-Corporation	Program development environment
KEE	Cf. Section 6.2		INTELLICORP	Shell
KES			Software Arch. and Engin. Inc., Arlington	Program development environment: FranzLISP
KL-ONE/ KL-TWO	Semantic networks and frames		BBN	Knowledge representation language
KNOW-LEDGE CRAFT			Carnegie Group Inc.	Program development environment: Symbolics and Texas Instr. LISP machines
KRL Knowledge representation Language	Frames		SLI + XEROX PARC	Knowledge representation language based on Interlisp

Name of Tool	Knowledge Representation	Special Application	Company/ Institution	Remarks
KS-300			TEKNOW-LEDGE, Inc.	Shell
LM	Frames	Programming of industrial robots		AI programming language
LOGLISP	List of objects		Syracuse University	AI programming language LISP dialect with PROLOG features
LOOPS	Cf. Section 6.4		XEROX PARC	Program development environment
LISP (COMMON LISP, ELISP, FRANZ-LISP, INTERLISP, INTERLISP-D, mu-LISP P-LISP, TLC-LISP, UCI-LISP, VLISP, ZETALISP)	Cf. Section 5.2		MIT	AI programming language
MBASE		Expert systems for mechanics, statistics, environmental problems	University of Edinburgh, Scotland	Shell implemented in PROLOG
MECS-AI		Medical diagnosis of time-dependent data	Toshiba R&D Center/Univ. of Tokyo Hosp.	Program development environment
MED1	Cf. Section 6.3		Kaiserslautern Univ.	Shell
MLSE	Production rules		Science Univ. of Tokyo	Program development environment

Name of Tool	Knowledge Representation	Special Application	Company/ Institution	Remarks
OMEGA			Delphia SpA.	Knowledge representation system for Symbolics, T.I., and LMI LISP machines, VAX Written in LISP
OPS (OPS4, OPS5, OPS7, OPS83)	Production rule systems	Production rule systems	CMU	AI programming language FranzLISP Note: R1 was written in OPS
OWL			MIT	AI programming language
PLANNER			MIT	AI programming language
POP-2			University of Edinburgh	AI programming language environment: DEC-10, TOPS-10, PDP11/UNIX
POP-11			Sussex University	AI programming language
POPLOG			Sussex University	Program development environment: VAX
PROLOG (C-PROLOG, MPROLOG)	Cf. Section 5.1		Marseille University	AI programming language
PS I		Program synthesis	SU	Program development environment
RLL	Inheritance mechanisms, slots and inheritance mechanisms		SU	Knowledge representation language RLL is an expert system implemented in Interlisp for the development of expert systems

Name of Tool	Knowledge Representation	Special Application	Company/ Institution	Remarks
ROSIE	Data- and event-triggered rule activation, concept hierarchies, inheritance mechanisms	Models of complex situations	RAND Corp., Santa Monica	Shell in Interlisp
ROSS	Hierarchical arrangement of object classes	Simulation of aerial combat	RAND Corp.	Object-oriented AI language
SAGE			SPL Research Center, England	Shell, production rules written in PASCAL, backward chaining environment: VAX/VMS, PDP/RSX
SAIL	Pattern recognition		SU	AI programming language
SCHEME			MIT	AI programming language
S.1	Cf. Section 6.1		TEKNOWLEDGE, Inc.	Shell
SMALLTALK	Objects that send and receive messages (passing messages)	Dynamic, non-sequential execution	XEROX PARC	AI programming language
TWAICE	Production rules, hierarchical object relationships through object tree, object-attribute value triple for representing facts	Consultation of diagnosis knowledge domains	Nixdorf, Paderborn	Shell in PROLOG environment: Nixdorf 8832 (UNIX), 8890 (VM)
UNITS	Rules, frames		SU	Knowledge representation language

A.2 Overview of Individual Expert Systems

This section contains a listing of known expert systems in alphabetical order.

The status of the individual systems of projects varies a great deal. Some are complete systems which have been implemented; others are smaller-scale research projects.

Abbreviations

L	Programming language/shell used
S̃	Size of system
CMU	Carnegie-Mellon-University
DEC	Digital Equipment Corporation
GMD	Gesellschaft für Mathematik und Datenverarbeitung
HP	Hewlett Packard
MIT	Massachusets Institute of Technology
PARC	Palo Alto Research Center
PMC	Pacific Medical Center, San Francisco
SRI	Stanford Research Institute
SU	Stanford University

Name of Expert System	Area of Application	Function/ Problem Class	Company/ Institution	Remarks
AALPS	Military affairs	Optimization of cargo/equip-ment loading in airplanes	U.S. Army	
AARON	Pictorial art	Design of abstract graphics	Univ. of Calif., San Diego	S: approx. 300 rules

Name of Expert System	Area of Application	Function/ Problem Class	Company/ Institution	Remarks
ABEL	Medicine	Diagnosis of metabolic disorders and acid-base imbalance	MIT	
ACE (Automated Cable Expertise)	Technology	Maintenance and trouble-shooting in telephone cables	Bell Lab.	L: Franz-LISP/OPS4 S: approx. 100 rules
ACE (Analysis of Complex Explanation)	Teaching	Analysis of complex explanations in CAI systems	University of Leeds	
ACT	Psychology	Modelling of human memory phenomena	CMU	
ADA* TUTOR	Software technology	Computer-supported instruction for learning programming language ADA	Computer Thought Corp.	
ADS	System design	Automated programming support for medical applications	IBM Scientific Center	
AIRPLAN	Aviation technology	Planning for starting and landing planes on aircraft carriers	CMU	L: OPS7
Air Traffic control	Aviation technology	Air traffic control	Univ. of Illinois	
AI-SPEAR	Computer technology	Fault diagnosis for magnetic tape devices	DEC	
ALVEN	Medicine	Determining the efficiency of the human heart	University of Toronto	

Name of Expert System	Area of Application	Function/ Problem Class	Company/ Institution	Remarks
AM/EU-RISKO	Mathematics	Generating new concepts and assertions	SU	S: approx. 350 rules
APE	Programming	Development of methods for coding extensive program knowledge	Bonn University	
APEX	Financial planning	Support for financial planners (advisors)	First Financial Planning Systems	
AQ/ ADVISE/ PLANT-ds/ PLANT-dc/ BABY	Biology	Diagnosis of plant diseases	University of Illinois	
ARS	Electronics	Analysis of electrical circuits	MIT	
ATTEND-ING	Medicine	Preoperative assessment of anesthesia	Yale University	
BACON/ GLAUBER/ DALTON	Physics	Finding regularities in databases, hypotheses generation	CMU	
BIRTH DEFECTS DIAGNOSIS	Medicine	Research and diagnosis of congenital diseases	MIT/Tufts New England Medical Center Hospital	
CAA	Cardiology	Detection of cardiac dysrhythmia and EKG anomalies	University of Toronto	L: PSN
CADHELP	CAD system	Generating intelligent explanation texts for graphic CAD systems	University of Connecticut	

Name of Expert System	Area of Application	Function/ Problem Class	Company/ Institution	Remarks
CALLISTO	Computer technology (chip design)	Managing tools for chip designers	DEC	
CASNET/ GLAU- COMA	Ophthalmology	Model of cause/effect mechanisms in glaucoma	Rutgers University, New Brunswick	
CATS-1/ DELTA	Engineering	Maintenance and trouble-shooting for locomotives	General Electric Co.	S: approx. 530 rules
CDX	System programming	Analysis of VMS dump files after a system crash	DEC	
CHEM- GUIDE	Training	Instruction in the use of a molecular synthesis program	Chemical Design, Oxford	
CHI	Software development	Support for programming, validation, and maintenance	Kestrel Institute, Palo Alto	
COMEX	Stock market sytem	Advice on commodities market regarding production and trade of agricultural products	MIT	L: FRL
COMPASS	Communications	Analysis of maintenance records for telecommunication switching networks	GTE	
CONAD	Computer technology	Configuration of computer sytems	Nixdorf, as per customer needs	

Name of Expert System	Area of Application	Function/ Problem Class	Company/ Institution	Remarks
CONSUL	Software development	Man-machine interface for interactive programming	University of Southern California, Marina Del Rey	L: KL-ONE
CRIB/ SOFTCRIB	Computer technology	Isolation of hardware/software faults	Brunel University	
CRYSALIS	Organic chemistry	Deriving the three-dimensional structure of unknown proteins from crystallographic X-ray photographs	SU	
CSS	Planning	Planning for relocation, new configuration, and new installation of large-scale computers	IBM	
DART	Computer technology	Fault diagnosis for computer systems in use	SU	L: EMYCIN S: approx. 190 rules
DAS-LOGIC	Electronics	Support for chip design	DEC	
DENDRAL/ CONGEN	Organic chemistry	Predicting structural formulae of organic compounds from measuring results of mass spectrographs, nuclear magnetic resonance spectra, and chemical analysis	SU	S: approx. 530 rules

Name of Expert System	Area of Application	Function/ Problem Class	Company/ Institution	Remarks
DEX.C3	Automotive engineering	Fault diagnosis in the automatic C3 transmission by FORD	GMD/FORD Company, Cologne	
DIGITALIS THERAPY ADVISOR	Medicine	Determining doses of cardiac glycosides	MIT	L: MACLISP
DIPMETER ADVISOR	Geology	Evaluation of measured values in petroleum deposit exploration	Schlumberger-Doll Res../ Schlumberger Offsh. Serv.	L: INTER-LISP S: approx. 90 rules
DISPATCH-ER	Planning	Delivery planning for robot parts	DEC	
DRILLING ADVISOR	Geology	Evaluation of measured values in petroleum prospecting	TEKNOW-LEDGE, Inc.	L: EMYCIN/ KS-300
EDDAS	Management	Guidance on disclosure of confidential company information	EPA	
EL	Electronics, Planning	Analysis of electric circuits	MIT	
ELAS	Geology	Interpretation of measured values in exploration	Amoco Production Research	L: EXPERT
EQUINOX	CAD/CAM	CAD/CAM-system with stored expert knowledge	Schlumberger	Interface to existing CAD/CAM systems
ESCORT	Production monitoring	Support of operators in monitoring and checking industrial plants	PA Computers and Telecomunication	Real-time system, Environment: XEROX 1108 with INTER-LISP-D + LOOPS
EXPLAN	Automotive engineering	Diagnosis of malfunctions in Otto engines	Batelle-Inst., Frankfurt	L: MYCIN

Name of Expert System	Area of Application	Function/ Problem Class	Company/ Institution	Remarks
FAULT-FINDER	Computer technology	Fault diagnosis in disk storage units	Nixdorf	
FINAN-CIAL ADVISOR	Management consulting	Advising on capital-intensive projects	Palladian Software	Hardware: Symbolics, Explorer
FOLIO	Financial advising	Financial advising system for portfolio management	Drexel Burnham Lambert/ SU	
GALEN	Medicine	Diagnosis of congenital heart disease in children	University of Minnesota	
GAMMA	Nuclear physics	Interpretation of gamma excitation spectra in unknown substances	Schlumberger-Doll Res.	
GEOX	Geology	Identification (detection) of minerals based on visual data	NASA	
GÚIDON/ NEOMY-CIN	Training	Model for teaching diagnostic skills	SU	
GUMMEX	Planning	Fully automatic generation of production plans for elastomer products	Batelle-Inst., Frankfurt	L: MYCIN
HEADMED	Medicine	Reducing drug medication in psychiatry	University of Texas	
HEARSAY I / HEARSAY II	Research	Speech recognition	University of Southern California	

Name of Expert System	Area of Application	Function/ Problem Class	Company/ Institution	Remarks
HYDRO	Hydrology	Solving problems with water resources	SRI	
IDT	System engineering	Fault diagnosis for computer hardware	DEC	L: OPS5
IMS	Production	Automation of industrial production (design, simulation, resource allocation)	CMU	L: SRL
IN-ATE	Technical diagnosis	Fault isolation in electrical circuits	U.S. Naval Research Lab.	
INTERNIST CADUCEUS	Internal medicine	Diagnosis for multiple disorders	University of Pittsburgh	
INFOMART ADVISOR	Consumer information	Guidance on computer purchases	Infomart, Dallas	
IPT	Computer technology	Diagnostic system for peripherals (currently, disk storage units)	Hewlett-Packard	S: approx. 550 rules
ISA	Planning	Production and delivery planning	DEC	
ISAAK	Physics	Solving physics text problems	University of Texas	
ITINERARY PLANNER	(Travel) planning	Travel planning (currently, rail connections in Australia only)	Expert-Systems International	Real-time system implemented in PROLOG
KLAUS	Teaching	Knowledge acquisition through verbal instructions	Artifical Intelligence Center, Menlo Park	

Expert Systems

Name of Expert System	Area of Application	Function/ Problem Class	Company/ Institution	Remarks
KNOBS/ SNUKA	Military	Executing aerial engagements in combat against enemy aircraft	MITRE Corp., Bedford	S: approx. 1400 FRL frames
KNOE-SPHERE	Entertainment, education, information, documentation	Electronically stored encyclopedia incorporating audio-visual means	ATARI	L: LISP
Kupplungs-experte (coupling expert)	Engineering	Calculates the optimal coupling for a given drive element	RWTH Aachen	L: PROLOG, Note: graphic representation of results possible
LDS	Legal matters	Determining damage claims under warranty	RAND Corp.	
LEGOL	Legal matters	Transforming new tax assessments to algorithmic rules	London School of Economics	
LIBRA	Programming	Analysis of program performance	CMU	
LINKMAN	Production control	Control and optimization of production processes	Blue Circle Technical	Hardware: PDP-11
LITHO	Geology	Interpretation of measured values in sample drilling for petroleum	Ecole Nationale Superiore des Telecomm./ Schlumberger, Montrouge	
LOPS	Mathematics	Automatic program synthesis	Munich University	

Name of Expert System	Area of Application	Function/ Problem Class	Company/ Institution	Remarks
MACSYMA	Mathematics	Formula manipulation (e.g., symbolic integration, non-numeric solutions to systems of equations)	MIT	
MDX	Medicine	Diagnosis of liver disorders	Ohio State University	
MENTOR	Engineering	Maintenance of air conditioning systems	Honeywell	
Meta-DENDRAL	Organic chemistry	Supplementary component (for rule generation in DENDRAL systems)	SU	
MICRO-FAST 2	Software design	Automatic generation of executable software	LEE Micromatics	Input: control flow charts
MICRO-SYNTHESE	Chemistry	Generation of synthesis trees of organic molecules	Ecole Nat. Sup. de Chimie de Paris	Hardware: Apple
MOLGEN	Biology	Planning genetic experiments	SU	
MYCIN	Internal medicine	Diagnosing infectious diseases and determining therapies	SU	S: approx. 500 rules PDP-11
NAVEX	Space technolgy	Monitoring the navigation system of the space shuttle	NASA	L: ART, environment: Symbolics 36770

Name of Expert System	Area of Application	Function/ Problem Class	Company/ Institution	Remarks	
NDS	Communications technology	Fault isolation in communications networks	SMART Syst. Techn./ Shell Dev. Comp.	S:	approx. 150 ARBY rules
NEXPERTS	Printing business	Generating page layout for newspapers	Composition Systems Inc., New York	L:	ART, environment: VAX
NTC	Communications technology	Fault analysis in Ethernet and DECnet networks	DEC		
NUCLEAR POWER PLANT CONSULTATION	Reactor technology	Monitoring reactors and operator training	Georgia Institute of Technology		
NUDGE	Planning	Assistant for scheduling meetings and conferences	MIT		
ODYSSEY	Planning	Travel and interface planning	XEROX PARC	L:	LISP
ONCOCIN	Medicine	Support in chemotherapy of cancer patients	SU		
PALLADIO	System design	Design of VLSI chips	SU/ XEROX PARC/ Fairchild AI Center		
PECOS	Programming	Implementation of abstract algorithms	SU	L: S:	INTER-LISP approx. 400 rules
PHI-NIX	Geology	Automatic programming system for rapid prototyping of special software (petroleum exploration)	Schlumberger-Doll Res.		

Name of Expert System	Area of Application	Function/ Problem Class	Company/ Institution	Remarks
PHOTO- LITHO- GRAPHY ADVISOR	Electronics	Fault diagnosis in chip produc- tion	Hewlett- Packard	S: approx. 218 backward- chaining rules
PICON	Process control	ON-LINE, real- time system for process control	Lisp Machines, Inc.	
PIES	Electronics	Fault Diagnosis in chip production	Fairchild	
PIP	Medicine	Model of clinical decision pro- cesses for anamnesis and diagnosis	MIT//Tufts University / New England Medical Center Hospital	
PLAN- POWER	Financial planning	Advising banks, insurance, and investment companies	Applied Expert Systems	Environment: XEROX 1186, S: approx. 6000 rules
PLE	Design	Design of pipelines for chemical plants	ICI Public Ltd./ Int. Term. Ltd.	
PRIDE	Engineering	Design and analysis of new copiers	XEROX	
PROGRAM- MERS APPREN- TICE	Programming	Interactive programming support	MIT	
PONTIUS-0	Airmanship	Learning flying techniques	MIT	
PROSPEC- TOR	Geology / mining	Exploring depo- sits of minerals (gold, uranium, molybdenum) and petroleum	SRI	S: approx. 1600 rules
PROSPEC- TOR WRITER	Medicine	Multi-modal prescription in cancer therapy	MIT	

Name of Expert System	Area of Application	Function/ Problem Class	Company/ Institution	Remarks
PSI	Programming	Automated program implementation	SU	
PUFF	Medicine	Diagnosis of pulmonary diseases	PMC/ SU	S:; approx. 250 rules
RABBIT	Databases	Intelligent assistant for database users	XEROX PARC	L: INTER-LISP-D/KL-ONE
RADEX	Medicine	Diagnosis by X-ray evaluation	Ohio State University	
REACTOR	Reactor technology	Monitor and crisis management	EG&G Idaho Inc.	
REDESIGN/ CRITTER	Circuit technology	Analysis, de-sign, and rede-sign of digital circuits	Rutgers University	
RHEUMA-TOLOGY CONSUL-TANT	Medicine	Diagnosis of rheumatic diseases	University of Missouri	L: EXPERT
RITA	System design	Implementing external user interfaces to external information systems	RAND Corp.	S: approx. 1000 rules
RIVER FLOOD EXPERT	Water resource management	Preventing floods when rivers carry high water	Universidad Politecnica Madrid	
RLL	System design	Expert systems for rapid expert system building	SU	

Name of Expert System	Area of Application	Function/ Problem Class	Company/ Institution	Remarks	
RX	Medicine	Gaining understanding of development, diagnosis, and treatment of chronic disorders (arteriosclerosis, cancer, hypertension, diabetes, arthritis)	SU		
R1/XCON	DP technology	Configuration of computer systems according to customer specifications	CMU/ DEC	L:	OPSS
				S:	approx. 1000 rules
SACON	Engineering	Analyzing the stability of technical structures (e.g., decks, bridges)	SU	S:	approx. 170 rules
SADD	Electronics	Structurecd modular design of digital circuits	University of Maryland		
SECS	Chemistry	Design of organic synthesis processes	University of California, Santa Cruz	L:	FORTRAN
SIUX	Database applications	Optimization of runtime performance	SIEMENS AG, München	L:	MED1
				S:	approx. 190 rules
SOPHIE	Electronics	System for teaching skills in electronic fault location	BNN/ XEROX PARC		
SPERIL	Building industry	Predicting structural damage caused by earthquakes	Purdue University		

Name of Expert System	Area of Application	Function/ Problem Class	Company/ Institution	Remarks
SPILLS	Crisis management	Assistance when dangerous chemicals are found in drain water	Oak Ridge National Lab.	
STAMMER2	Naval systems	Identifying objects (war-ships)	Naval Ocean System Center, San Diego	S: approx. 170 rules
STEAMER	Steam engine technology	CAI system for teaching marine personnel steam engine technology	Naval Personal Research&Deve-lopment Center	
SU/X	Military systems / signal processing	Identifying and tracing moving objects by evaluating sonograms	SU	
SYN	Electronics	Circuit design	XEROX PARC	
SYNCHEM	Chemistry	Finding work-able and effi-cient synthesis procedures for complex organic compounds	SUNY	L: PL/1
TALEM	Electronics	Integrated circuit design	CMU	L: OPS5 S: approx. 1500 rules
TAXAD-VISOR	Financial affairs	Financial advisor for investment planning	University of Illinois	S: EMYCIN

Name of Expert System	Area of Application	Function/ Problem Class	Company/ Institution	Remarks
TAXMAN		Automated programming support for medical applications	IBM Scientific Center	L: AIMDS
TEIRESIAS	System design	Simplifying interactive knowledge transfer from expert to knowledge base (interactive debugging, manipulation of control structure by metarules)	SU/ MIT	S: 55,000 36-bit words
TIMM/ TUNER	System programming	Diagnosis and optimization of performance in VAX systems	General Research Corporation of California	in FORTRAN
TVX	Teaching	Teaching the use of VMS operating systems	DEC	
VERIFY	Electronics	Checking digital circuit designs	Fairchild Lab. for AI Research	L: PROLOG
VM	Medicine	Control of "iron lung"	PMC/ SU	
VMS ADVISOR/ WIZARD	Software engineering	Help for users of VMS operating systems	University of Pennsylvania	L: Franz-LISP/ KL-ONE
VT	Engineering	Configuration of new elevator systems	Westinghouse	
WHEAT COUNSEL-LOR	Agriculture	Advice on controlling "disease" in cereal plants	ICI	

Name of Expert System	Area of Application	Function/ Problem Class	Company/ Institution	Remarks
XPRT-SYSTEM	Programming	Collection of LISP programs for support in expert systems implementation	MIT/ Schlumberger-Doll Res.	L: LISP
XSEL/ XCITE/ XCALIBUR	Computer technology	Customer-specific configuration of (VAX) computer systems	CMU/ DEC	
YES/MVS	System programming	Supervisor of MVS operating system	IBM	

A.3 Glossary

acquisition component

> Component of an expert system; used by the → knowledge engineer for building the → knowledge base.

algorithm

> A set of processing steps for solving a specific problem according to a precisely defined procedure.

artificial intelligence (AI)

> A broad definition for new techniques of formal logic, new search strategies, and methods of knowledge representation in computer programs to imitate human problem solving processes. Application areas include natural language systems, computer vision and image interpretation systems, robotics, expert systems.

backtracking

> As defined for PROLOG, cancelling values linked to variables if → unification is not possible. The → inference mechanism then attempts to find another rule for achieving unification. This procedure of revoking value links, i.e., backing up, to facilitate selection of another rule is called backtracking.

backward chaining

> Problem-solving method based on a hypothesis. All rules in the knowledge base leading to this goal are selected, followed by a check to determine whether the known facts satisfy the conditions and the goal can be realized, or whether applicable rules exist that can be used for satisfying the conditions. The same procedure is used for the conditions of these rules.

blackboard

> Work area in an expert system which is used by the inference mechanism to record solution paths and results that can be considered during the consultation in progress.

bottom-up theory
> An AI research application intended to implement adaptive networks based on technical imitations of the human brain.

breadth-first search
> All options at a branching point are followed; for example, all rules available at this point are applied before moving down to the next level in the decision tree.

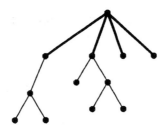

computer vision and image interpretation
> Interpreting images by means of precisely defined processes.

declarative programming paradigm
> Description of knowledge independent of the processing method used. Strict adherence to the paradigm does not permit any procedural sequences to be formulated, unlike conventional data processing, which uses procedural programming (→ procedural programming paradigm).

depth-first search
> Selection and use of *one* option at a branching point so that the next level in the decision tree can be reached quickly.

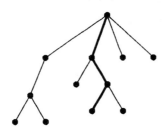

domain

A narrowly defined problem area.

expert system

Software which emulates the problem-solving behavior of an expert. Expert systems can be used to store the expert knowledge for a restricted subject field and to solve a problem in this area by logical inferencing.

expertise

Expert knowledge needed for solving specific problems.

explanation component

Feature of an expert system. The explanation component of an expert system must be able to trace the solution steps and supply reasons why a solution path was taken. In addition, it supplies explanations to system questions and deduced facts and can specify object attributes.

fact

A statement considered to be valid; a fact exists in an expert system if it is included in the → knowledge base.

(to) fire

If the premise of a rule is satisfied based on the facts and its conclusion part has been implemented, the rule is said to fire (→production rule).

forward chaining

Problem-solving method in which the knowledge base is searched for the rules associated with known facts and the action part of these rules is executed until the solution is reached or no more rules can be applied.

frame

> A formal data structure for → knowledge representation. A frame is used for describing objects and object classes; initially, it is a structured data frame which is filled with contents during processing. Several frames with identical structures may have different contents.

functional programming paradigms

> A solution is reached by the exclusive use of functions. An executed function supplies a value as the result, which is further processed by the calling function.

inference mechanism

> Part of an expert system that draws inferences from a knowledge base according to a fixed problem-solving method. The functions of the inference mechanism include controlling the actions between the individual parts of the expert system, determining the time for and the type of rule processing, controlling the dialogue with the users.

inference strategy

> Method used by the inference mechanism in problem solving, e.g., backward chaining.

inheritance

> Object-oriented programming lets an object inherit attributes of a "parent" object. Information about similar objects is stored only once and made available to other objects through inheritance.

knowledge base

> The components of an expert system that contain the konwledge (→expertise).
> The knowledge base not only stores individual facts; it also includes complex objects, their attributes, relationships between objects, and rules for processing knowledge and for deriving new knowledge from existing knowledge, i.e. heuristics.

knowledge engineer
Questions the expert to establish the knowledge required for problem solving, structures this knowledge, and includes it in the → knowledge base.

knowledge representation
A method for representing formalized and structured knowledge in expert systems. For example, methods in knowledge representation that can support knowledge structuring are → production rules, → semantic networks, → frames.

LISP (Acronym for LISt Processing)
Programming language for list-processing; also used for developing expert systems. The emphasis is on processing symbols and structures.

natural language systems
Designation for systems that use algorithms for syntactic, semantic, and pragmatic analyses of messages, i.e. for generating natural language.

object-oriented programming
Programming procedure that describes information as objects. The objects are determined by their attributes and responses.

predicate calculus
Formal method of knowledge representation.
Formal language with its own syntax and grammar that can evaluate logical statements and draw inferences for generating other statements.

procedural programming paradigms
Solving a programming problem by specifying the solution paths as individual steps, as opposed to → functional and → declarative programming paradigms.

production rules
Method of → knowledge representation in the knowledge base. These rules are used to represent knowledge as *If premises, Then conclusion and/or action.*

production system

System consisting of → production rules.

PROLOG

PROgramming in LOGic; an imlementation of 1st order predicate calculus as a programming language.

rapid prototyping

Software development method which facilitates rapid design by using particularly efficient development systems and short implementation and test cycles.

robotics

Research in techniques to add "intelligence" to the performance of robots.

rule-based systems

→ expert systems.

semantic networks

A method used to represent knowledge of object relationships. The nodes of a semantic network represent objects, the links describe relationships between objects.

However, the semantic network does not provide any information about network processing. Processing rules must be explicitly formulated.

shell

Software tool that supports the work of the → knowledge engineer. Shells contain components of an expert system, but not the knowledge base. Some are simply tools for structuring knowledge, i.e., programs for representing associated knowledge. Others provide one or more knowledge representation mechanisms and possibly inference mechanisms. Some also offer extensive control options or support the interface design.

top-down theory

>An AI research application based on the assumption that human intelligence can best be simulated by complex programs that copy human thought processes.

unification

>As defined for PROLOG, unification is the process of achieving equivalent structures by linking values to variables.

Expert Systems

References

[1] Rich, Elain. **Artificial Intelligence.** MacGraw Hill, 1983.

[2] Savory, Stuart, E. **Künstliche Intelligenz und Expertensysteme: Artificial Intelligence – State of the Art 1984.** Oldenbourg, 1985.

[3] Winograd, T. **Understanding Natural Language.** Academic Press, 1972.

[4] Bobrow and Collins. **Representation and Understanding: Studies in Cognitive Science.** Academic Press, 1975.

[5] Winston, P. **The Psychology of Computer Vision.** 1975.

[6] Clocksin, W.F., and C.S. Mellish. **Programming in Prolog.** 2nd ed. Berlin, Heidelberg: Springer Verlag, 1984.

[7] Kowalski, R. "Algorithm = Logic + Control." **Communications of the ACM,** 22/7 (July 1979).

[8] Hayes-Roth, S., et al. **Building Expert Systems.** Addison-Verlag, 1983.

Bibliography

Bachant, J. and J. Mc Dermott. "R1 Revisited: Four Years in the Trenches." **The AI Magazine,** Fall 1984, p. 21 ff.

Banerjee, N., et al. "Worauf Sie beim Aufbau eines Expertensystems achten müssen." **State of the Art,** 1 (1986), p. 11 ff.

Bobrow, Daniel G., and Mark Stefik (XEROX PARC). **The LOOPS Manual.** December 1983.

Bonnet, A. **Artificial Intelligence - Promise and Performance.** Englewood Cliffs, 1985.

Buchanan, B., and E. Shortliffe, eds. **Rule-Based Expert Systems.** Adison-Wesley Publ. Co., 1984.

Büttel, I. "Expertensysteme." **Der Elektroniker,** 3 (1986), p. 72 ff.

Büttel, I., and K.Bauer. "Expertensystem-Technik." Internal SIEMENS Study, 1985.

Davis, R. and D. Lenat. **Knowledge-Based Systems in Artificial Intelligence.** New York, 1982.

Goodman, H. "Expert Systems." Seminar. Munich, 1985.

Harmon, P., and D. King. **Expert Systems – Artificial Intelligence in Business.** New York, 1985.

INTELLICORP. **KEE Version 2.1, Software DevelopmentSystem: User's Manual.** July 1985.

_____. **KEE Version 2.1, Software Development System: Rule System2 Reference Manual.** October 1985.

_____. **KEE Version 2.1, Software Development System: Active Images Manual.** October 1985.

Kahn, G., and S. Nolan. "A Foundation for Knowledge Acquisition." **The AI Magazine,** Fall 1984, p. 61 ff.

Lenat, D. "Eurisco: A Program That Learns New Heuristics and Domain Concepts." **Artificial Intelligence,** 1983, p. 61 ff.

Mittal, S. "Knowledge Acquisition from Multiple Experts." IEEE: Workshop on Principles of Knowledge-Based Systems. Denver, 1983, p. 75 ff.

Newell, A. "The Knowledge Level." **Artificial Intelligence,** 1 (1982), p. 87 ff.

O'Shea, T., and M. Eisenstadt. **Artificial Intelligence Tools, Techniques and Applications.** New York, 1985.

Puppe, F. **Expertensysteme: Informatik Spektrum.** 1986

_____. "MED1: A Heuristic Diagnosis System with Efficient Control Structure." Memo SEKI-83-04, Kaiserslautern University. Thesis, 1983.

Rose, F. **Ins Herz des Verstandes. Auf dem Weg zur Künstlichen Intelligenz.** Rowohlt-Verlag, 1986.

Stefik, M. "The Organization of Expert Systems. A Tutorial." **Artificial Intelligence,** 1982.

Wahlster, W. "Wissenbasierte Systeme im Büro. Grundlagen, Funktionsweise, Anwendungen von Expertensystemen." Seminar, 1985.

Index